PRAXIS® 5362 English to Speakers of Other Languages

Willow L. Taylor

This page is intentionally left blank.

iii

This page is intentionally left blank.

Table of Content

This page is intentionally left blank.

Chapter 1 – Questions

QUESTION 1

Which of the following phonological concepts is most likely to affect an English language learner's pronunciation of the word "school"?

A. Allophones
B. Phonemes
C. Minimal pairs
D. Syllable stress

Answer:

QUESTION 2

An ESOL teacher notices that a student is consistently adding "-ed" to irregular verbs, such as saying "buyed" instead of "bought." This demonstrates a challenge with:

A. Derivational morphemes
B. Inflectional morphemes
C. Free morphemes
D. Bound morphemes

Answer:

QUESTION 3

An ESOL teacher is working with a group of students who are constructing sentences using the verb "to be." One student creates the sentence: "She am happy." This error most likely relates to difficulties with:

A. Subject-verb agreement
B. Verb tense
C. Direct objects
D. Indirect speech acts

Answer:

QUESTION 4

An ESOL teacher notices that a student consistently replaces the /θ/ sound (as in "think") with the /s/ sound (as in "sink"). This is an example of difficulties with:

A. Phonemic stress
B. Minimal pairs
C. Voicing
D. Consonant clusters

Answer:

QUESTION 5

When teaching English pronunciation, which concept focuses on the varying degrees of stress placed on different syllables within a word?

A. Syllable structure
B. Intonation
C. Suprasegmentals
D. Articulation

Answer:

QUESTION 6

An ESOL teacher is helping students differentiate between the /p/ and /b/ sounds. Which activity would be most effective for achieving this goal?

    A.   Focusing on tongue placement for /p/ and lip vibration for /b/
    B.   Demonstrating how to pronounce /p/ and /b/ in isolation
    C.   Discussing the history of English phonology
    D.   Practicing /p/ and /b/ in sentences with different stress patterns

Answer:

QUESTION 7

An ESL teacher notices that a student, who recently moved to the country, is struggling to participate actively in classroom discussions. The student appears hesitant and avoids eye contact during conversations. Which individual factor might be affecting the student's language acquisition?

    A.   Lack of motivation
    B.   Sociocultural background
    C.   Previous language exposure
    D.   Cognitive processing speed

Answer:

QUESTION 8

An ESL teacher is working with a group of adolescent students who have experienced disruptions in their education due to frequent relocations. This mobility has led to gaps in their academic development. How might these academic factors affect their L2 acquisition?

    A.   Accelerate language acquisition due to exposure to diverse linguistic environments
    B.   Impede language acquisition by promoting a fixed mindset about learning
    C.   Enhance language acquisition by fostering cognitive flexibility
    D.   Hinder language acquisition by affecting their vocabulary retention

Answer:

QUESTION 9

An ESL teacher is planning lessons for a class of adult learners. The students come from various professional backgrounds, including healthcare, engineering, and business. How might these sociopolitical factors influence their language-learning needs?

    A.   Professional backgrounds may lead to stronger oral communication skills but weaker reading skills.
    B.   Sociopolitical factors are unlikely to impact language-learning needs in an adult classroom.
    C.   Cultural backgrounds may cause resistance to group activities in the classroom.
    D.   Different professional backgrounds may result in varied language demands and registers.

Answer:

QUESTION 10

In a classroom of ESL learners, a student frequently takes notes during lectures, organizes study groups, and reflects on their learning progress. This student often adjusts their learning approach based on their self-assessment. Which type of language-learning strategy is this student employing?

    A.   Cognitive strategy
    B.   Metacognitive strategy
    C.   Social/communicative strategy
    D.   Mnemonic strategy

Answer:

QUESTION 11

An ESL teacher notices that a group of students is struggling to remember new vocabulary words. To support their vocabulary development, the teacher designs activities where students associate new words with familiar images and personal experiences. Which type of language-learning strategy is the teacher promoting?

    A.   Cognitive strategy
    B.   Metacognitive strategy
    C.   Social/communicative strategy
    D.   Mnemonic strategy

Answer:

QUESTION 12

An ESL teacher is observing a pair of students engaged in a role-play activity. They take on different roles and engage in a simulated conversation using target language structures. This activity encourages negotiation of meaning and interaction. Which type of language-learning strategy is being utilized?

    A.   Cognitive strategy
    B.   Metacognitive strategy
    C.   Social/communicative strategy
    D.   Mnemonic strategy

Answer:

QUESTION 13

An ESL teacher is working with a group of adult learners who have immigrated to a new country. Some students are highly proficient in their native language and are struggling to accept their developing language skills in the host country. Which sociopolitical factor might contribute to this challenge?

    A.   Linguistic assimilation
    B.   Cultural relativity
    C.   Cultural hierarchy
    D.   Acculturation

Answer:

QUESTION 14

An ESL teacher is working with a class of elementary school students. Some students come from families where their home language is spoken exclusively, while others come from bilingual households. How might these individual factors influence the students' L2 acquisition?

    A.   Students from bilingual households will struggle with cognitive overload due to dual language exposure.
    B.   Students from monolingual households will have stronger L2 vocabulary due to focused language exposure.
    C.   Individual language exposure will not significantly impact L2 acquisition in young learners.
    D.   Students from bilingual households may show greater language flexibility and metalinguistic awareness.

Answer:

QUESTION 15

An ESL teacher is working with a student who has recently experienced a traumatic event in their home country before moving to a new one. The student displays signs of anxiety and difficulty concentrating in class. How might this individual factor affect the student's L2 acquisition and development?

    A.   Trauma is unlikely to impact language acquisition as language development is a separate cognitive process.
    B.   Trauma may hinder the student's emotional readiness for language acquisition but not cognitive aspects.
    C.   Trauma may affect the student's cognitive processing and emotional well-being, thus impacting language acquisition.
    D.   Trauma will only affect the student's L2 pronunciation but not other language skills.

Answer:

QUESTION 16

Which of the following instructional strategies is most effective for teaching ESL students about different genres of written discourse?

    A.   Providing a list of grammar rules specific to each genre.
    B.   Engaging students in reading and analyzing authentic texts from different genres.
    C.   Conducting rote memorization exercises for vocabulary related to various genres.
    D.   Focusing solely on oral communication to improve writing skills.

Answer:

QUESTION 17

When teaching oral discourse, how can ESL teachers promote effective communication and interaction in the classroom?

    A.   Encouraging students to stick to their native language during group discussions.
    B.   Providing a list of pre-prepared responses for students to use in conversations.
    C.   Creating opportunities for collaborative discussions and debates on relevant topics.
    D.   Discouraging the use of gestures and body language during verbal communication.

Answer:

QUESTION 18

An ESL teacher notices that one of their students frequently interrupts others while they are speaking. Which instructional approach would be most effective in addressing this pragmatics issue?

    A.   Ignoring the behavior as it might be culturally acceptable in the student's home country.
    B.   Providing corrective feedback and explicitly teaching turn-taking and conversational rules.
    C.   Asking the student to stop speaking altogether during classroom discussions.
    D.   Avoiding group discussions to prevent the student from interrupting others.

Answer:

QUESTION 19

Which of the following is an example of a formal register that ESL students should be familiar with to succeed in academic settings?

    A.   Slang language used among friends during informal gatherings.
    B.   Technical jargon specific to a particular industry.
    C.   Casual language commonly used in online chat and social media.
    D.   Colloquial language used in daily conversations with close family members.

Answer:

QUESTION 20

As an ESL teacher, you want to improve your students' ability to summarize texts accurately. Which activity would be most effective in achieving this goal?

    A.   Asking students to read a text and then write a summary in their native language.
    B.   Providing students with a completed summary and asking them to memorize it.
    C.   Guiding students through the process of identifying key points and creating their own summaries.
    D.   Assigning lengthy texts for reading without any follow-up activities.

Answer:

QUESTION 21

When teaching oral discourse, how can you encourage ESL students to develop their critical thinking skills during class discussions?

    A.   Discouraging students from asking follow-up questions to maintain the flow of the discussion.
    B.   Allowing students to express their opinions freely without offering any evidence or justification.
    C.   Facilitating debates on controversial topics, where students must support their arguments with evidence.
    D.   Providing model answers and requiring students to repeat them during discussions.

Answer:

QUESTION 22

How can ESL teachers promote effective written discourse when working with beginner-level students?

    A.   Assigning complex writing tasks right from the start to challenge students.
    B.   Providing sentence stems and writing templates to help students structure their writing.
    C.   Focusing solely on grammar exercises and neglecting actual writing practice.
    D.   Discouraging students from seeking help or feedback from peers.

Answer:

QUESTION 23

Which of the following strategies is most effective in helping ESL students understand implied meanings in English conversations?

    A.   Encouraging students to avoid ambiguous language and only use straightforward expressions.
    B.   Providing a list of idiomatic expressions and asking students to memorize their meanings.
    C.   Exposing students to authentic conversations and discussing the context and implied meanings.
    D.   Asking students to rely solely on dictionaries to interpret idiomatic expressions.

Answer:

QUESTION 24

An ESL teacher notices that some students tend to apologize excessively, even when the situation does not call for it. How can the teacher address this pragmatics issue effectively?

    A.   Discouraging students from apologizing altogether to reduce linguistic interference.
    B.   Explicitly teaching students the appropriate use of apologies and other speech acts.
    C.   Ignoring the excessive apologies as they are a form of cultural expression.
    D.   Encouraging students to avoid using apologies in any situation.

Answer:

QUESTION 25

How can ESL teachers help students develop their understanding of conversational implicatures and indirect speech acts?

- A. Providing a list of common indirect expressions and their literal translations.
- B. Discouraging students from using indirect speech acts to avoid misunderstandings.
- C. Engaging students in role-playing activities where they practice using indirect speech acts.
- D. Instructing students to only use direct and explicit language in all communication.

Answer:

QUESTION 26

Why is it essential for ESL teachers to introduce students to different English language variations and registers?

- A. To discourage students from using colloquial language in any context.
- B. To encourage students to imitate native speakers' accents for better pronunciation.
- C. To equip students with the language skills necessary for different social and professional settings.
- D. To discourage students from communicating with individuals from different language backgrounds.

Answer:

QUESTION 27

Which of the following statements about dialects is correct?

- A. Dialects are incorrect forms of a language and should be avoided in all contexts.
- B. Dialects are used exclusively by specific ethnic groups and are not widely understood.
- C. Dialects are regional variations of a language and are equally valid forms of communication.
- D. Dialects should be used only when speaking with close family members to maintain cultural identity.

Answer:

QUESTION 28

When teaching ESL students about language registers, which of the following would be the most appropriate order for instruction?

- A. Casual register, Formal register, Neutral register
- B. Neutral register, Casual register, Formal register
- C. Formal register, Casual register, Neutral register
- D. Formal register, Neutral register, Casual register

Answer:

QUESTION 29

A group of ESL students is struggling with reading comprehension in English. As an ESL teacher, what approach would be most beneficial to support their L2 literacy development?

- A. Advise students to solely focus on reading in their L1 (native language) to improve L2 reading skills.
- B. Encourage students to read extensively in English, regardless of the complexity of the texts.
- C. Provide explicit instruction on reading strategies and support students in transferring these skills from L1 to L2.
- D. Advise students to skip reading altogether and focus on other language skills.

Answer:

QUESTION 30

What is the role of L1 literacy in the development of L2 literacy skills among ESL students?

    A.   L1 literacy has no impact on L2 literacy development; they are independent processes.
    B.   L1 literacy can hinder L2 literacy development, leading to more challenges in learning English.
    C.   L1 literacy provides a strong foundation and can positively influence L2 literacy development.
    D.   L1 literacy is only relevant if the L1 and L2 languages share similar writing systems.

Answer:

QUESTION 31

What are some challenges that ESL students may face during the process of acquiring literacy in English?

    A.   The challenges are mainly related to pronunciation and speaking skills, not literacy.
    B.   ESL students may find it difficult to learn the alphabet and basic phonics.
    C.   ESL students are generally proficient in English literacy due to immersion experiences.
    D.   Challenges are limited to grammatical rules and syntax, not literacy skills.

Answer:

QUESTION 32

An ESL teacher has a mixed-level class with beginning, intermediate, and advanced English language learners. How can the teacher differentiate instruction effectively to meet the diverse language proficiency levels?

    A.   Focus only on advanced-level content, as intermediate and beginning students will catch up eventually.
    B.   Provide the same instructional materials and activities for all students to maintain fairness.
    C.   Tailor instruction to target each group's proficiency level, using appropriate materials and tasks.
    D.   Encourage advanced-level students to support their peers without direct teacher intervention.

Answer:

QUESTION 33

Which of the following characteristics is typical of an intermediate English language proficiency level?

    A.   Ability to use complex academic vocabulary and understand specialized texts.
    B.   Comfort with simple social interactions, but difficulty with abstract or complex topics.
    C.   Fluency in writing formal essays with minimal errors in grammar and mechanics.
    D.   Mastery of advanced grammatical structures, but challenges with basic conversational exchanges.

Answer:

QUESTION 34

What is one key difference between social-language development and academic-language development in second-language acquisition?

    A.   Social-language development involves learning slang and colloquial expressions, while academic-language development focuses on formal language use.
    B.   Social-language development is necessary for everyday interactions, while academic-language development is solely required for classroom activities.
    C.   Social-language development occurs in informal settings, while academic-language development takes place in structured educational contexts.
    D.   Social-language development primarily involves listening and speaking, while academic-language development encompasses reading and writing as well.

Answer:

QUESTION 35

A group of ESL students comes from diverse linguistic backgrounds with varying levels of L1 literacy. As an ESL teacher, how can you utilize this diversity to enhance L2 literacy development?

A. Separate students into homogeneous groups based on their L1 literacy levels for targeted instruction.
B. Focus solely on improving L1 literacy skills to support the transfer to L2 literacy development.
C. Encourage peer collaboration and discussions among students to foster cross-linguistic learning.
D. Ignore the students' L1 literacy backgrounds and focus on teaching English in isolation.

Answer:

QUESTION 36

During a reading comprehension lesson, an ESL teacher notices that a group of students struggles to understand the main idea of the text. What strategy would be most effective in improving their L2 literacy skills?

A. Provide a translated version of the text in the students' L1 to aid comprehension.
B. Simplify the text by removing challenging vocabulary and complex sentence structures.
C. Model and explicitly teach strategies such as identifying key information and making inferences.
D. Suggest the students practice reading aloud to improve their pronunciation and comprehension.

Answer:

QUESTION 37

As an ESL teacher, you notice that some students exhibit strong L1 literacy skills but struggle to transfer these skills to their L2 literacy development in English. What could be a possible reason for this challenge?

A. The students' L1 and L2 languages have similar writing systems, leading to interference.
B. The students' L1 literacy skills are not well-developed, causing difficulties in both languages.
C. The students might not be motivated to improve their L2 literacy skills due to cultural factors.
D. The students' L1 and L2 languages have significant differences in grammar and syntax.

Answer:

QUESTION 38

An ESL teacher has a class with students at different English language proficiency levels, including beginning, intermediate, and advanced. How can the teacher ensure meaningful and inclusive classroom discussions that accommodate all students?

A. Encourage only advanced-level students to actively participate in discussions to maintain accuracy.
B. Design tasks and questions that challenge beginning students and exclude advanced-level students.
C. Provide opportunities for all students to contribute by using varying levels of linguistic support.
D. Divide students into separate groups based on proficiency levels for exclusive discussions.

Answer:

QUESTION39

Which of the following characteristics is typical of a beginning English language proficiency level?

A. Ability to comprehend complex academic lectures and textbooks with minimal support.
B. Proficiency in using academic vocabulary and writing formal research papers.
C. Fluency in everyday conversations and expressing basic needs and preferences.
D. Competency in understanding nuanced language and figurative expressions.

Answer:

QUESTION 40

How can ESL teachers effectively support intermediate-level students in developing their academic-language proficiency?

    A.   Assigning tasks with complex academic vocabulary without any guidance or support.
    B.   Providing opportunities for peer tutoring where intermediate students teach beginners.
    C.   Integrating academic language instruction into content-based lessons and assignments.
    D.   Exclusively focusing on grammar instruction to improve academic writing skills.

Answer:

QUESTION 41

Which of the following best describes the role of the first language (L1) in second language (L2) acquisition?

    A.   L1 hinders the acquisition of L2.
    B.   L1 has no influence on L2 acquisition.
    C.   L1 can facilitate the acquisition of L2.
    D.   L1 and L2 are completely independent and don't affect each other.

Answer:

QUESTION 42

What is the term used to describe the ability of an individual to speak three languages?

    A.   Bilingualism
    B.   Trilingualism
    C.   Multilingualism
    D.   Polyglotism

Answer:

QUESTION 43

Which of the following best describes heritage language learning?

    A.   Learning a new language for travel purposes.
    B.   Learning a language that is not commonly spoken in the learner's country.
    C.   Learning a language spoken by one's ancestors or in the family but not actively used in the community.
    D.   Learning the official language of a country for educational purposes.

Answer:

QUESTION 44

Which of the following statements best describes the role of first language (L1) literacy in second language (L2) literacy development?

    A.   L1 literacy has no impact on L2 literacy development.
    B.   L1 literacy accelerates L2 literacy development, making it faster.
    C.   L1 literacy can serve as a foundation for L2 literacy development.
    D.   L1 literacy creates confusion and hinders L2 literacy development.

Answer:

QUESTION 45

What is a common challenge related to literacy development in English language learners?

    A.   Faster literacy development compared to native English speakers.
    B.   Limited access to reading materials and resources in the native language.
    C.   Lack of motivation to learn English due to cultural barriers.
    D.   Absence of prior literacy skills in the native language.

Answer:

QUESTION 46

What is one of the major concepts related to literacy development in English language learners?

    A.   Graphology
    B.   Semantics
    C.   Phonetics
    D.   Syntax

Answer:

QUESTION 47

Which of the following is a characteristic feature of a beginning English language learner (ELL)?

    A.   Able to engage in complex academic discussions with native speakers.
    B.   Has a wide range of academic vocabulary.
    C.   Relies heavily on nonverbal communication to express ideas.
    D.   Demonstrates native-like pronunciation and fluency.

Answer:

QUESTION 48

What is the term used to describe the social language used in everyday, casual interactions?

    A.   Bilingual language
    B.   Academic language
    C.   Communicative language
    D.   Basic Interpersonal Communication Skills (BICS)

Answer:

QUESTION 49

Which of the following best describes an intermediate English language learner (ELL)?

    A.   Capable of understanding complex academic texts and writing essays fluently.
    B.   Struggles to communicate basic needs and understand simple questions.
    C.   Has limited vocabulary and relies on basic sentence structures.
    D.   Can participate in group discussions but struggles with reading comprehension.

Answer:

QUESTION 50

Maria is an ESL teacher working in a diverse urban school. She has a class with students from various cultural and language backgrounds. One day, during a class discussion, two students from different regions engage in a conversation using their regional dialects. Other students seem confused and ask Maria to intervene. How should Maria handle this situation?

    A. Correct the students' dialects and instruct them to use standard English.
    B. Ask the students to switch to their native languages to avoid confusion.
    C. Use this opportunity to explain the concept of language variations and dialects.
    D. Suggest that the students refrain from speaking in their regional dialects in the classroom.

Answer:

QUESTION 51

In a suburban ESL classroom, there is a student who speaks English fluently but uses informal language and slang excessively, even in academic discussions. This student's communication style is affecting their performance in formal writing tasks. How can the teacher address this issue?

    A. Encourage the student to communicate only in their native language.
    B. Correct the student's informal language use in front of the class to set an example.
    C. Provide explicit instruction on when and where informal language is appropriate.
    D. Ignore the issue and focus on other language skills to avoid embarrassing the student.

Answer:

QUESTION 52

An ESL teacher is planning a lesson on English language variations and registers. The class consists of adult learners with varying language proficiency levels. How can the teacher make the lesson engaging and relevant for all students?

    A. Use only formal academic texts to teach language variations.
    B. Assign complex language exercises to challenge all students equally.
    C. Incorporate authentic materials and real-life situations that use different registers.
    D. Focus solely on the teacher's native dialect for consistency.

Answer:

QUESTION 53

A new ESL student, Juan, recently arrived in the country and has little exposure to the English language. The teacher notices that Juan's native language (Spanish) influences his pronunciation of English words, making it challenging for others to understand him. How can the teacher address this issue effectively?

    A. Encourage Juan to use his native language more often to improve pronunciation.
    B. Correct Juan's pronunciation in front of the class to make him aware of the errors.
    C. Provide pronunciation drills and practice with minimal pair exercises.
    D. Ignore the pronunciation issues and focus on other language skills.

Answer:

QUESTION 54

Sofia, an ESL teacher, has a diverse class with students from different cultural backgrounds. She notices that some students with stronger first language (L1) literacy skills tend to excel in reading and writing tasks in English, while others struggle. How can Sofia support students with weaker L1 literacy skills?

A. Separate the students with weaker L1 literacy skills from the rest of the class for focused instruction.
B. Assign more reading and writing tasks to students with weaker L1 literacy skills to improve their skills.
C. Provide scaffolding and support, such as graphic organizers and vocabulary aids, for reading and writing tasks.
D. Discourage the use of L1 and require students to rely solely on English during class activities.

Answer:

QUESTION 55

An ESL teacher is working with a group of adult learners who are at an advanced English language proficiency level. The learners have expressed their desire to enhance their language skills beyond the academic context. How can the teacher cater to their needs effectively?

A. Focus solely on grammar and academic vocabulary to prepare for formal exams.
B. Encourage learners to use only academic language and avoid informal language.
C. Integrate authentic materials and real-world tasks to promote practical language use.
D. Limit the use of technology and multimedia as it may distract adult learners.

Answer:

QUESTION 56

As an ESL teacher, you have a class with students from different cultural backgrounds. During a group discussion, one student uses a regional dialect that is not widely understood by the rest of the class. What approach should you take to address this situation effectively?

A. Correct the student's use of the regional dialect immediately.
B. Ask the student to refrain from participating in the discussion.
C. Use this as a teachable moment to discuss language variations and registers.
D. Switch the discussion topic to avoid further confusion.

Answer:

QUESTION 57

In an ESL class, you have a student who speaks English fluently but uses informal language and slang even during formal presentations. The student's peers find it challenging to take the presentation seriously. How can you help the student improve their language use in formal contexts?

A. Require the student to avoid using any slang in all situations.
B. Advise the student to use formal language only during presentations.
C. Provide explicit instruction on the appropriate use of language registers.
D. Limit the student's participation in formal speaking tasks.

Answer:

QUESTION 58

You are planning an ESOL lesson for a group of adult learners. The class includes individuals with varying levels of language proficiency and cultural backgrounds. How can you make the lesson on language variations engaging and relevant to all learners?

A. Use only academic texts to maintain consistency in language use.
B. Assign language exercises based on the teacher's dialect.
C. Incorporate authentic materials that showcase diverse language variations.
D. Focus solely on the learners' native languages to build confidence.

Answer:

QUESTION 59

You have a student, Anna, who has recently migrated to an English-speaking country. Anna's English language proficiency is still developing, and she often makes grammar errors that reflect the structures of her native language. How can you assist Anna in improving her English language skills?

    A.   Discourage Anna from using her native language to focus solely on English.
    B.   Immediately correct Anna's grammar errors to reinforce correct usage.
    C.   Provide targeted language feedback and explain the differences between her native language and English.
    D.   Advise Anna to avoid speaking until she feels more confident in English.

Answer:

QUESTION 60

In your ESL class, you have a group of students who come from different language backgrounds. Some students have a strong foundation in their first language, while others are beginners. How can you utilize the knowledge of L1 in L2 acquisition to enhance your teaching approach for this diverse group?

    A.   Encourage students with a strong L1 foundation to assist beginners in translating.
    B.   Focus solely on the students' L1 to ensure consistent language use in the classroom.
    C.   Utilize students' L1 knowledge to make connections and facilitate L2 learning.
    D.   Discourage the use of L1 during class to promote immersion in the target language.

Answer:

QUESTION 61

You have an ESL class with students at different language proficiency levels. Some students are at the beginning stage, while others are more advanced. How can you tailor your language instruction to meet the needs of these diverse learners effectively?

    A.   Provide separate language instruction for beginners and advanced students.
    B.   Assign advanced reading materials to challenge all students equally.
    C.   Differentiate instruction by using various language resources and tasks.
    D.   Limit language instruction to activities that focus solely on grammar.

Answer:

QUESTION 62

What is the term for the smallest unit of sound in a language?

    A.   Morpheme
    B.   Phoneme
    C.   Syntax
    D.   Semantics

Answer:

QUESTION 63

Which of the following describes the process of acquiring a language naturally, often during early childhood, without explicit instruction?

    A.   Code-switching
    B.   Bilingualism
    C.   Language acquisition
    D.   Linguistic relativity

Answer:

QUESTION 64

What term describes the rules governing the order of words in a sentence to create meaningful communication?

A. Phonology
B. Pragmatics
C. Syntax
D. Morphology

Answer:

QUESTION 65

When a child overgeneralizes a language rule, such as saying "goed" instead of "went," it demonstrates:

A. Overextension
B. Underextension
C. Overgeneralization
D. Assimilation

Answer:

QUESTION 66

The study of how language is used in different social contexts and how language varies across different groups is known as:

A. Semiotics
B. Pragmatics
C. Sociolinguistics
D. Psycholinguistics

Answer:

QUESTION 67

Maria, a new student, has recently moved to the country and is just beginning to learn English. She can say a few basic phrases like "hello" and "thank you," but struggles to hold longer conversations. What English language proficiency level would you classify Maria as?

A. Intermediate
B. Beginning
C. Advanced
D. Proficient

Answer:

QUESTION 68

Ahmed is an immigrant student who has been learning English for a year. He can participate in classroom discussions, express his opinions, and write short paragraphs. Which English language proficiency level is Ahmed likely to be at?

A. Advanced
B. Intermediate
C. Proficient
D. Beginning

Answer:

QUESTION 69

Elena is a student who can read academic textbooks, write essays, and give presentations in English. She also easily interacts with native speakers in social situations. What English language proficiency level does Elena demonstrate?

    A. Beginning
    B. Intermediate
    C. Proficient
    D. Advanced

Answer:

QUESTION 70

Carlos, a high school student, comes from a background where his native language is rarely spoken in his new country. Despite his efforts, he struggles with both academic and social English. What individual factor might be affecting Carlos's language acquisition?

    A. Socioeconomic status
    B. Age of acquisition
    C. Cognitive ability
    D. Native language influence

Answer:

QUESTION 71

Fatima, a newcomer to the country, faces prejudice and discrimination due to her cultural background. She often feels anxious and excluded in social settings. How might sociopolitical factors impact her L2 acquisition?

    A. Positive motivation
    B. Enhanced cognitive ability
    C. Language aptitude
    D. Negative affective filter

Answer:

QUESTION 72

Raj is a university student from a non-English-speaking country. He values education and has a strong desire to excel academically. How might his academic motivation affect his L2 acquisition and development?

    A. Decrease cognitive ability
    B. Impede language exposure
    C. Enhance language learning
    D. Increase native language interference

Answer:

QUESTION 73

Lila, an ESL student, consistently uses flashcards, watches English movies, and practices speaking with native speakers to improve her language skills. What type of language-learning strategy is Lila employing?

    A. Cognitive strategies
    B. Metacognitive strategies
    C. Social/communicative strategies
    D. Socioaffective strategies

Answer:

QUESTION 74

Javier is a language learner who reflects on his learning progress, sets goals, and adjusts his study techniques accordingly. What category of language-learning strategies does Javier's behavior belong to?

- A. Cognitive strategies
- B. Metacognitive strategies
- C. Social/communicative strategies
- D. Compensation strategies

Answer:

QUESTION 75

Anna, an ESL teacher, encourages her students to work on collaborative projects, engage in role-playing, and participate in group discussions. What type of language-learning strategy is Anna promoting?

- A. Cognitive strategies
- B. Metacognitive strategies
- C. Social/communicative strategies
- D. Socioaffective strategies

Answer:

QUESTION 76

Which of the following individual factors can significantly impact L2 acquisition?

- A. The availability of language learning resources
- B. The current economic status of the country
- C. The native language spoken by the learner
- D. The length of the school day

Answer:

QUESTION 77

In an academic setting, what factor is likely to hinder L2 development for a student?

- A. Being surrounded by native speakers of the target language
- B. Receiving regular feedback and encouragement from the teacher
- C. Having limited opportunities for meaningful language practice
- D. Engaging in extracurricular language exchange activities

Answer:

QUESTION 78

Which sociopolitical factor can positively impact L2 acquisition in a community?

- A. Strict language policies that discourage multilingualism
- B. Educational programs that promote bilingualism and multiculturalism
- C. Limited access to technology and digital resources
- D. High levels of linguistic isolation from other communities

Answer:

QUESTION 79

Which language-learning strategy involves analyzing and identifying personal learning strengths and weaknesses?

A. Social interaction with native speakers
B. Memorizing vocabulary lists
C. Metacognitive self-assessment
D. Repetitive grammar drills

Answer:

QUESTION 80

When learning new vocabulary, which strategy involves creating mental connections between known and new words?

A. Mnemonic devices
B. Rote memorization
C. Repeating words aloud
D. Using translation apps

Answer:

QUESTION 81

Which social/communicative language-learning strategy promotes fluency through spontaneous interaction with others?

A. Reading extensively in the L2
B. Participating in language exchange programs
C. Taking grammar-focused online courses
D. Watching subtitled movies in the target language

Answer:

QUESTION 82

Sarah is an ESL teacher working with a group of young learners who are struggling with pronunciation. She notices that some students have difficulty differentiating between the /l/ and /r/ sounds, leading to miscommunication in the classroom. How can Sarah address this issue effectively?

A. Correct each mispronunciation immediately to ensure students learn the correct sounds.
B. Ignore the mispronunciations as they will likely outgrow the problem over time.
C. Provide explicit instruction on tongue placement and airflow for /l/ and /r/ sounds.
D. Ask students to practice pronouncing minimal pairs of /l/ and /r/ sounds independently.

Answer:

QUESTION 83

Juan is an ESL teacher working with a diverse group of adult learners. He notices that some students have difficulty producing the /θ/ and /ð/ sounds, such as in "think" and "this," which affects their overall intelligibility. How can Juan support these students in improving their pronunciation?

A. Encourage students to avoid using words with /θ/ and /ð/ sounds to minimize miscommunication.
B. Explain that the /θ/ and /ð/ sounds are not essential for effective communication in English.
C. Use tongue twisters containing /θ/ and /ð/ sounds as a fun and challenging pronunciation exercise.
D. Provide explicit instruction on tongue placement and airflow for /θ/ and /ð/ sounds and practice them in context.

Answer:

QUESTION 84

Emma, an ESL teacher, is working with a group of young learners who often struggle with blending sounds to form words. They frequently mispronounce words like "cat" as "cot" or "sip" as "ship." How can Emma help her students develop their blending skills?

A. Encourage students to repeat individual sounds separately to reinforce their phonemic awareness.
B. Focus only on reading comprehension activities to improve blending skills indirectly.
C. Provide opportunities for students to listen to and repeat simple words and sentences.
D. Avoid using any phonics-based activities as they might confuse the students further.

Answer:

QUESTION 85

Alex is an ESL teacher working with a group of intermediate-level adult learners. Some students are struggling with understanding and using English prefixes and suffixes. How can Alex support these students in developing their morphological awareness?

A. Focus on teaching complex grammar rules to help students grasp the use of prefixes and suffixes.
B. Provide a list of common prefixes and suffixes without explaining their meanings.
C. Engage students in activities where they analyze the meanings and functions of prefixes and suffixes in context.
D. Advise students to avoid using words with prefixes and suffixes until they become more proficient.

Answer:

QUESTION 86

Maria is an ESL teacher working with young learners who are beginning to read and write in English. She notices that some students struggle with irregular plurals, such as "mice" and "feet." How can Maria help her students grasp irregular plural forms?

A. Advise students to focus on memorizing a list of irregular plural forms without explanation.
B. Teach students only regular plural rules to avoid confusion with irregular forms.
C. Use engaging activities that involve exposure to and practice with irregular plurals in context.
D. Encourage students to skip using plural forms until they reach an advanced level of English proficiency.

Answer:

QUESTION 87

Mark, an ESL teacher, is working with advanced-level adult learners who want to improve their writing skills. Some students struggle with sentence structure and often create run-on sentences. How can Mark help these students improve their syntax and sentence construction?

A. Provide students with lengthy reading materials to encourage them to write longer sentences.
B. Advise students to avoid complex sentence structures to prevent run-on sentences.
C. Teach students about punctuation marks and how to use them to create clear and concise sentences.
D. Engage students in activities that focus on sentence combining and sentence variety.

Answer:

QUESTION 88

Rachel is an ESL teacher working with a group of intermediate-level learners. Some students struggle with understanding word meanings and context. How can Rachel help her students develop their semantic understanding and vocabulary skills?

A. Advise students to rely solely on dictionaries to look up word meanings.
B. Encourage students to memorize long lists of vocabulary without using them in context.
C. Engage students in activities that focus on using context clues to infer word meanings.
D. Advise students to avoid using unfamiliar words in their writing and speaking.

Answer:

QUESTION 89

John, an ESL teacher, is working with a group of advanced-level adult learners who need to improve their public speaking skills. Some students struggle with maintaining coherence and structure during their presentations. How can John help these students enhance their oral discourse skills?

- A. Advise students to read their presentations verbatim to ensure accuracy.
- B. Provide students with pre-written speeches to deliver during their presentations.
- C. Teach students about effective organizational patterns and transitions for speeches.
- D. Encourage students to use complex sentence structures to impress the audience.

Answer:

QUESTION 90

Anna is an ESL teacher working with a group of intermediate-level learners who struggle with writing cohesive paragraphs. Many students have difficulty linking ideas together to form a unified text. How can Anna help her students improve their written discourse skills?

- A. Advise students to avoid using linking words to keep their paragraphs concise.
- B. Provide students with pre-written paragraphs to copy and submit as their own work.
- C. Teach students about different types of linking devices and how to use them effectively.
- D. Encourage students to use overly complex vocabulary to enhance their writing.

Answer:

QUESTION 91

What is the primary goal of creating a culturally inclusive learning community in an ESL classroom?

- A. To eliminate all cultural differences among students
- B. To promote language learning exclusively through textbooks
- C. To celebrate and leverage students' diverse cultural backgrounds
- D. To prioritize academic achievement over cultural awareness

Answer:

QUESTION 92

In a culturally inclusive ESL classroom, why is it important to incorporate diverse perspectives and materials in the curriculum?

- A. To make the curriculum more difficult and challenging
- B. To avoid any potential conflicts related to cultural differences
- C. To enhance students' critical thinking and understanding of the world
- D. To limit students' exposure to different cultural viewpoints

Answer:

QUESTION 93

How can an ESL teacher foster a sense of belonging and inclusivity in a culturally diverse classroom?

- A. By encouraging students to only interact with peers from the same cultural background
- B. By avoiding discussions about cultural topics to prevent misunderstandings
- C. By creating opportunities for students to share and learn from each other's cultures
- D. By assigning grades based solely on language proficiency

Answer:

QUESTION 94

Which ESOL program model focuses on gradually transitioning students from their native language to English instruction?

- A. Immersion program
- B. Dual-language program
- C. Sheltered instruction program
- D. Transitional bilingual program

Answer:

QUESTION 95

What is a key characteristic of the dual-language program model?

- A. It exclusively teaches students in their native language
- B. It aims to replace students' native language with English
- C. It promotes bilingualism and biliteracy in both English and another language
- D. It focuses solely on academic achievement without considering language development

Answer:

QUESTION 96

Which ESOL program model is designed to immerse students in an English-speaking environment regardless of their language proficiency?

- A. Pull-out program
- B. Content-based ESL program
- C. Bilingual education program
- D. Immersion program

Answer:

QUESTION 97

Which teaching approach emphasizes the direct teaching of grammar rules and focuses on accuracy in language production?

- A. Communicative Language Teaching (CLT)
- B. Task-Based Language Teaching (TBLT)
- C. Audio-Lingual Method
- D. Whole Language Approach

Answer:

QUESTION 98

Which teaching approach encourages authentic communication and situational language use to enhance language learning?

- A. Silent Way
- B. Grammar-Translation Method
- C. Task-Based Language Teaching (TBLT)
- D. Direct Method

Answer:

QUESTION 99

Which historical teaching approach was criticized for neglecting learners' communicative competence and focusing too much on memorization?

- A. Silent Way
- B. Grammar-Translation Method
- C. Natural Approach
- D. Direct Method

Answer:

QUESTION 100

What is the primary purpose of using formative assessments in ESOL instruction?

- A. To assign final grades and evaluate student performance
- B. To provide feedback to students and guide instruction
- C. To measure overall language proficiency at the end of the year
- D. To determine eligibility for ESOL programs

Answer:

QUESTION 101

When planning differentiated ESOL instruction, what does differentiation refer to?

- A. Teaching only the most advanced students in the class
- B. Providing the same instructional approach to all students
- C. Adapting instruction to meet the diverse needs of students
- D. Focusing solely on grammar and vocabulary instruction

Answer:

QUESTION 102

How can ESOL teachers use summative assessments effectively in their instruction?

- A. To determine daily classroom activities and tasks
- B. To evaluate the effectiveness of a single instructional lesson
- C. To make long-term decisions about curriculum and instruction
- D. To replace formative assessments in ongoing instruction

Answer:

QUESTION 103

In your ESL classroom, you have students from various cultural backgrounds. You notice that some students are hesitant to share their opinions in class discussions. What approach could you take to address this situation?

- A. Encourage those students to conform to the dominant cultural communication style
- B. Avoid involving students in discussions to prevent discomfort
- C. Implement group discussions that allow for different communication preferences
- D. Discourage students from expressing opinions to avoid potential conflicts

Answer:

QUESTION 104

In a diverse ESL classroom, you observe that students from collectivist cultures tend to collaborate more effectively in group projects, while individualist culture students prefer working alone. How can you address this difference to promote effective collaboration?

    A.   Assign projects based solely on individual work
    B.   Provide opportunities for students to work with peers from the same cultural background
    C.   Teach all students to adapt to the collectivist approach
    D.   Develop strategies that allow both individual and group work, respecting diverse preferences

Answer:

QUESTION 105

You are planning a cultural awareness activity in your ESL class. One of your students expresses discomfort with participating, as they feel it may perpetuate stereotypes. How could you address this concern?

    A.   Insist that the student participate to promote cultural awareness
    B.   Modify the activity to ensure it avoids reinforcing stereotypes
    C.   Remove the student from the activity to prevent any discomfort
    D.   Cancel the activity altogether to avoid potential conflicts

Answer:

QUESTION 106

One of your ESL students is experiencing low self-esteem due to instances of racism and discrimination in and out of school. How could you support this student's language development and overall well-being?

    A.   Advise the student to ignore the incidents and focus solely on language learning
    B.   Offer additional academic support to compensate for the emotional challenges
    C.   Create a safe and supportive classroom environment, addressing the emotional impact of discrimination
    D.   Suggest the student switch to a different school to avoid further challenges

Answer:

QUESTION 107

You have a student who is struggling with English language acquisition. You suspect that the student's lack of progress might be related to negative stereotypes about their cultural background. How could you address this situation?

    A.   Confirm the stereotypes with the student to encourage them to improve
    B.   Provide the student with extra language worksheets to catch up
    C.   Challenge the stereotypes and provide positive reinforcement and encouragement
    D.   Advise the student to only interact with peers from their own cultural background

Answer:

QUESTION 108

A new ESL student is hesitant to participate in classroom activities due to the fear of being stigmatized for their accent. How could you promote a positive environment that encourages the student to engage confidently?

    A.   Discourage the student from speaking until their accent improves
    B.   Highlight the student's accent as a unique cultural trait
    C.   Provide opportunities for the student to share their culture and experiences
    D.   Isolate the student from group activities to avoid potential embarrassment

Answer:

QUESTION 109

In your ESL class, you have students from high-context and low-context cultures. How could you address potential misunderstandings and promote effective communication?

    A. Encourage students to avoid communication with peers from different cultural backgrounds
    B. Teach all students to adopt a single communication style to avoid confusion
    C. Raise awareness of different communication styles and provide strategies for effective cross-cultural communication
    D. Assign separate activities for students from different cultural backgrounds

Answer:

QUESTION 110

You notice that some ESL students are more comfortable with direct communication, while others prefer indirect communication. How could you create a balanced communication environment that respects diverse preferences?

    A. Discourage indirect communication styles to promote consistency
    B. Adopt only the direct communication style to avoid confusion
    C. Acknowledge and value both direct and indirect communication styles, providing opportunities for practice
    D. Assign separate communication styles to different groups of students

Answer:

QUESTION 111

During a classroom discussion, one ESL student frequently nods their head while another student avoids eye contact. How could you interpret and address these nonverbal cues in a culturally sensitive manner?

    A. Assume the nodding student agrees with the discussion and the other student disagrees
    B. Disregard the nonverbal cues and focus solely on verbal responses
    C. Seek opportunities to discuss cultural differences in nonverbal communication and encourage both students to share their thoughts
    D. Assign grades based solely on verbal participation to avoid potential biases

Answer:

QUESTION 112

In your ESL class, you have students from various cultural backgrounds. You notice that some students are hesitant to share their opinions in class discussions. What approach could you take to address this situation?

    A. Encourage those students to conform to the dominant cultural communication style
    B. Avoid involving students in discussions to prevent discomfort
    C. Implement group discussions that allow for different communication preferences
    D. Discourage students from expressing opinions to avoid potential conflicts

Answer:

QUESTION 113

In a culturally inclusive ESL classroom, you encounter a conflict between two students due to misunderstandings arising from their different cultural norms. How could you address this conflict while fostering cultural awareness and understanding?

    A. Ignore the conflict and hope it resolves on its own
    B. Punish both students for not understanding each other's perspectives
    C. Facilitate a respectful dialogue between the students, highlighting the cultural differences and promoting empathy
    D. Separate the students to prevent any future conflicts

Answer:

QUESTION 114

During a classroom activity, you notice that some ESL students are more comfortable with individual tasks, while others prefer collaborative work. How could you design activities that cater to different cultural preferences while promoting inclusivity?

    A.   Assign only individual tasks to avoid potential conflicts
    B.   Insist that all students engage in collaborative activities to promote teamwork
    C.   Offer a variety of activity options, allowing students to choose based on their preferences
    D.   Divide the class into separate groups based on cultural background

Answer:

QUESTION 115

What is a potential challenge that may arise due to cross-cultural differences in the classroom?

    A.   Increased collaboration among students
    B.   Enhanced understanding of global perspectives
    C.   Misinterpretation of nonverbal cues
    D.   Improved classroom management

Answer:

QUESTION 116

How can understanding the values and beliefs of students' cultures benefit the classroom environment?

    A.   It encourages students to conform to the teacher's culture.
    B.   It helps create an inclusive and supportive learning environment.
    C.   It eliminates cultural diversity in the classroom.
    D.   It leads to a one-size-fits-all teaching approach.

Answer:

QUESTION 117

What is an effective strategy for addressing cross-cultural differences in the classroom?

    A.   Ignoring cultural differences to promote equality
    B.   Implementing standardized assessments for all students
    C.   Encouraging students to assimilate into the dominant culture
    D.   Incorporating culturally responsive teaching practices

Answer:

QUESTION 118

How can cultural identity positively influence language development in second language learners?

    A.   It may lead to the loss of the first language.
    B.   It can create a sense of belonging and motivation to learn the second language.
    C.   It causes difficulties in adapting to the dominant culture.
    D.   It hinders the development of cognitive abilities.

Answer:

QUESTION 119

What is the potential impact of racism and discrimination on language learning and academic achievement of English language learners?

  A. Racism and discrimination have no effect on language learning.
  B. They can enhance self-esteem and confidence in language learning.
  C. They may result in feelings of exclusion and hinder academic progress.
  D. Racism and discrimination only affect students with advanced language proficiency.

Answer:

QUESTION 120

How can ESL teachers address the effects of stereotyping in the language learning environment?

  A. Promote and reinforce stereotypes to build cultural awareness.
  B. Ignore stereotypes and focus solely on language instruction.
  C. Challenge stereotypes through diverse and inclusive teaching materials.
  D. Encourage students to conform to the stereotypes of their cultural group.

Answer:

QUESTION 121

What is a potential challenge in cross-cultural communication?

  A. Assuming all cultures have identical communication styles
  B. Adopting a direct communication approach with all individuals
  C. Using complex language to ensure clarity in communication
  D. Avoiding adaptation of communication style to fit cultural norms

Answer:

QUESTION 122

Which approach is recommended for effective cross-cultural communication?

  A. Emphasizing your cultural norms and values
  B. Avoiding eye contact to show respect in all cultures
  C. Using humor and sarcasm to lighten the conversation
  D. Being open-minded and respectful of cultural differences

Answer:

QUESTION 123

What is a potential consequence of misinterpreting nonverbal cues in cross-cultural communication?

  A. Enhanced mutual understanding between cultures
  B. Increased trust and rapport between individuals
  C. Misunderstandings and conflicts in communication
  D. Strengthening of cultural stereotypes

Answer:

QUESTION 124

Maria is an ESL teacher working in a diverse school with a large population of English language learners (ELLs). The school district offers two ESOL program models: pull-out and inclusion. In the pull-out model, ELLs attend separate ESL classes for a portion of the day, while in the inclusion model, ELLs are integrated into mainstream classrooms with additional language support. Maria is tasked with recommending a program model for a group of recently arrived ELLs with limited English proficiency. What factors should Maria consider when making her recommendation?

    A. The convenience for teachers and administrators
    B. The availability of resources for each program model
    C. The language development needs and English proficiency levels of the students
    D. The popularity of the program model among parents

Answer:

QUESTION 125

John, an ESL teacher, is reviewing research on the effectiveness of different ESOL program models. He comes across a study that compares the outcomes of the dual-language immersion program with the transitional bilingual program. The study indicates that students in the dual-language immersion program outperform their peers in academic achievement and bilingual proficiency. Why might this be the case?

    A. The transitional bilingual program focuses more on native language development.
    B. The dual-language immersion program prioritizes English language learning over the native language.
    C. The dual-language immersion program provides opportunities for students to use both languages for academic content.
    D. The transitional bilingual program requires students to transition to English-only instruction quickly.

Answer:

QUESTION 126

Lisa is an ESL coordinator responsible for selecting an appropriate ESOL program model for a high school with a diverse ELL population. The school currently uses the sheltered instruction approach, which provides modified content instruction for ELLs in mainstream classrooms. However, Lisa is considering implementing the newcomer program, which offers specialized English language instruction for recently arrived ELLs before transitioning them to regular classes. What are potential benefits of the newcomer program?

    A. Students can receive content instruction in their native language.
    B. It helps ELLs develop language skills more quickly.
    C. The program is less expensive to implement compared to other models.
    D. ELLs are immediately integrated into regular classrooms.

Answer:

QUESTION 127

Jennifer, an ESL teacher, is exploring different ESOL teaching approaches to improve her instructional practices. She comes across two methodologies: the Grammar-Translation method and the Communicative Language Teaching (CLT) approach. Jennifer notices that the Grammar-Translation method focuses on explicit grammar instruction and translation exercises, while CLT emphasizes communication and interaction. Which method is more aligned with current language teaching research and best practices?

    A. The Grammar-Translation method, as it provides a structured approach to language learning.
    B. The CLT approach, as it promotes meaningful communication and language use.
    C. Both methods are equally effective and widely used in ESOL classrooms.
    D. Neither method is supported by current research, and they should be avoided.

Answer:

QUESTION 128

A group of ESL teachers is discussing the Audiolingual Method and the Task-Based Language Teaching (TBLT) approach. The Audiolingual Method emphasizes the repetition of dialogues and pattern drills, while TBLT centers on completing meaningful tasks that require language use. The teachers are trying to determine which method would better suit their students, who are preparing for everyday communication in English. What would be a key consideration in making this decision?

    A.   The ease of implementation for the teachers
    B.   The availability of materials and textbooks for each method
    C.   The students' specific language learning goals and needs
    D.   The popularity of each method among other schools

Answer:

QUESTION 129

Daniel, an ESL teacher, is researching past and current ESOL teaching approaches. He comes across the Direct Method, which encourages students to learn the target language directly without translation, and the Natural Approach, which emphasizes immersion and meaningful language use. Daniel wonders which approach would be better for developing students' oral language skills. What evidence supports the effectiveness of one of these approaches?

    A.   The Direct Method, as it provides a systematic approach to language learning.
    B.   The Natural Approach, as it promotes language acquisition through immersion and meaningful communication.
    C.   Both approaches have equal research support for oral language skill development.
    D.   Neither approach is effective for developing oral language skills.

Answer:

QUESTION 130

Which criterion is most important when selecting instructional resources for English Language Learners (ELLs)?

    A.   The resource's popularity among other teachers.
    B.   The resource's alignment with the students' cultural background and language proficiency.
    C.   The resource's price and affordability.
    D.   The resource's availability at the nearest bookstore.

Answer:

QUESTION 131

What is an effective method for adapting a complex reading passage for beginner ELLs?

    A.   Remove all challenging vocabulary to simplify the text.
    B.   Replace the passage with a shorter text on a different topic.
    C.   Provide a glossary with definitions for key vocabulary words.
    D.   Increase the length of the reading passage to provide more context.

Answer:

QUESTION 132

Which of the following best describes a key aspect of designing ESOL instructional resources?

    A.   Developing resources based on teacher preferences and expertise.
    B.   Creating materials exclusively in the students' native language.
    C.   Aligning resources with language proficiency levels and learning objectives.
    D.   Using a one-size-fits-all approach for diverse groups of ELLs.

Answer:

QUESTION 133

What is a key strategy for using authentic materials to support language and content instruction for ELLs?

- A. Simplify the authentic materials to remove cultural references.
- B. Replace authentic materials with traditional textbooks.
- C. Choose authentic materials that match students' interests and experiences.
- D. Provide authentic materials without any scaffolding.

Answer:

QUESTION 134

How can teachers promote language development while using multimedia resources in the ESOL classroom?

- A. Allow students to watch videos without any language-related activities.
- B. Use multimedia resources with excessive visual effects and background music.
- C. Encourage students to engage in discussions and reflections after using multimedia resources.
- D. Provide printed transcripts and expect students to read along silently.

Answer:

QUESTION 135

What is a valuable strategy for promoting academic language development in the ESOL classroom?

- A. Focusing solely on everyday conversational language.
- B. Integrating academic vocabulary across content areas.
- C. Relying on rote memorization of grammar rules.
- D. Using only written texts for language practice.

Answer:

QUESTION 136

What is a primary benefit of using language learning apps in the ESOL classroom?

- A. Reducing student engagement and motivation.
- B. Providing limited opportunities for independent practice.
- C. Allowing personalized and self-paced learning experiences.
- D. Limiting access to authentic language input.

Answer:

QUESTION 137

How can video conferencing tools be beneficial in the ESOL classroom?

- A. Limiting opportunities for real-time communication and collaboration.
- B. Allowing students to practice language skills in authentic contexts.
- C. Restricting teacher-student interactions to pre-recorded videos.
- D. Eliminating opportunities for distance learning.

Answer:

QUESTION 138

What is a critical consideration when incorporating online resources in the ESOL classroom?

- A. Relying solely on one type of online resource to address all language skills.
- B. Avoiding the use of interactive multimedia for language practice.
- C. Restricting students' access to online resources outside of class.
- D. Using online resources that are not compatible with different devices.

Answer:

QUESTION 139

Maria is an ESL teacher working with a diverse group of ELLs with varying language proficiency levels. She wants to introduce a new topic on environmental conservation. Which instructional strategy would be most effective in supporting her students' language and content learning?

- A. Assigning a lengthy reading passage on environmental conservation and expecting students to summarize it in writing.
- B. Using multimedia resources, such as videos and interactive websites, to engage students and facilitate discussions about environmental issues.
- C. Providing only written worksheets on the topic to ensure students focus solely on improving their reading comprehension.
- D. Conducting lectures in the teacher's native language to ensure all students understand the content.

Answer:

QUESTION 140

In an ESL classroom with limited technology resources, Sarah wants to incorporate technology to support her ELLs' language skills. What strategy can she use to achieve this goal effectively?

- A. Assigning regular writing assignments without any digital support.
- B. Using smartphones to play language learning games during class breaks.
- C. Creating a classroom blog where students can share their thoughts and experiences.
- D. Relying solely on traditional printed textbooks for language instruction.

Answer:

QUESTION 141

Javier's ESL classroom has limited access to physical textbooks and traditional resources. He wants to provide his ELLs with opportunities for independent learning and practice. What technology-based solution can he implement?

- A. Encouraging students to use translation apps for language practice.
- B. Integrating online language learning platforms with interactive exercises.
- C. Limiting students' technology use to prevent distractions during class.
- D. Distributing photocopied worksheets as the primary instructional resource.

Answer:

QUESTION 142

As an ESL teacher, Mark is exploring ways to use technology to enhance vocabulary instruction for his ELLs. Which technology-based strategy would be most effective in supporting his students' vocabulary development?

- A. Using flashcards with printed words and images.
- B. Utilizing digital flashcards with audio pronunciations.
- C. Conducting vocabulary quizzes only using paper and pencil.
- D. Encouraging students to memorize vocabulary lists.

Answer:

QUESTION 143

Sophia wants to leverage technology to enhance listening and speaking skills for her ELLs. How can she achieve this goal using available classroom technology?

A. Assigning listening exercises and expecting students to write responses on paper.
B. Conducting group discussions with students taking notes on their laptops.
C. Using video conferencing tools to connect with native English speakers for conversations.
D. Giving out printed transcripts and asking students to read along with audio recordings.

Answer:

QUESTION 144

In a technology-rich ESL classroom, Emma is keen on promoting creativity and collaboration among her ELLs. How can she effectively use technology to achieve this objective?

A. Allowing students to play video games during leisure time.
B. Integrating online collaborative platforms for group projects and discussions.
C. Encouraging students to spend more time on social media platforms.
D. Using e-books for independent reading without group activities.

Answer:

QUESTION 145

As an ESL teacher, Julie is designing a formative assessment to gauge her students' language progress throughout the semester. Which approach would best demonstrate the reliability of this assessment?

A. Giving the same test at the beginning and end of the semester to compare results.
B. Administering different versions of the test to different student groups.
C. Using a test that aligns with the students' language proficiency levels.
D. Assigning a subjective writing prompt to measure students' creativity.

Answer:

QUESTION 146

In a diverse ESOL classroom, Mr. Johnson wants to ensure that the assessments he uses are valid and fair for all students. What should he consider when evaluating the validity of his assessments?

A. Administering only multiple-choice questions for objective measurement.
B. Using a mix of assessment types to address various language skills.
C. Setting the same pass mark for all students regardless of their proficiency levels.
D. Grading assessments based on students' effort rather than accuracy.

Answer:

QUESTION 147

Maria is an ESL coordinator responsible for evaluating the effectiveness of an annual proficiency test used in the ESOL program. Which quality indicator should she focus on to determine the test's reliability?

A. The number of students who achieve a passing score.
B. The correlation between the test scores and students' classroom performance.
C. The variety of questions types included in the test.
D. The use of the same test format in previous years.

Answer:

QUESTION 148

Which assessment type is best suited for measuring a student's ability to engage in real-life communication situations, such as conversations and interactions?

A. Multiple-choice test
B. Oral proficiency interview
C. True/false test
D. Fill-in-the-blanks test

Answer:

QUESTION 149

In order to determine the consistency and stability of an assessment instrument over time, what quality indicator is being measured?

A. Validity
B. Reliability
C. Authenticity
D. Constructability

Answer:

QUESTION 150

Which type of assessment focuses on observing students' behavior and performance in real-world contexts to gather information about their language skills and abilities?

A. Summative assessment
B. Formative assessment
C. Performance-based assessment
D. Diagnostic assessment

Answer:

QUESTION 151

What is the primary purpose of formative assessment in an ESOL classroom?

A. Assign final grades to students
B. Assess students' language proficiency levels
C. Guide instructional decisions and provide feedback
D. Measure students' knowledge at the end of a unit

Answer:

QUESTION 152

When communicating assessment results to stakeholders, which strategy promotes a better understanding of the data and its implications?

A. Using technical jargon and specialized terminology
B. Presenting raw scores without context
C. Providing clear explanations and visual representations
D. Only sharing positive outcomes

Answer:

QUESTION 153

What type of assessment is typically used to evaluate students' overall language proficiency at the end of an instructional period and is often used for accountability purposes?

- A. Diagnostic assessment
- B. Summative assessment
- C. Formative assessment
- D. Performance-based assessment

Answer:

QUESTION 154

Which benefit is associated with using multiple measures of assessment for English Language Learners?

- A. Simplifies the assessment process for teachers
- B. Reduces the need for ongoing assessment
- C. Provides a more comprehensive view of students' abilities
- D. Focuses solely on language proficiency without considering content knowledge

Answer:

QUESTION 155

How can teachers align assessments with relevant language and content-area standards and objectives?

- A. By designing assessments that are unrelated to standards
- B. By using standardized tests exclusively
- C. By considering the language demands of content areas
- D. By avoiding any connection between assessments and curriculum

Answer:

QUESTION 156

Why is ongoing assessment important in ESOL instruction?

- A. It simplifies the grading process for teachers
- B. It ensures that students only receive summative assessments
- C. It allows teachers to track students' progress and adjust instruction
- D. It eliminates the need for communicating assessment results to stakeholders

Answer:

QUESTION 157

What is a limitation of using standardized tests to measure English Language Learners' content knowledge?

- A. They are too easy for ELL students
- B. They don't provide valid results for ELL students
- C. They only measure language proficiency, not content knowledge
- D. They are more suitable for ELL students than native speakers

Answer:

QUESTION 158

When interpreting standardized assessment results for ELLs, what consideration is important due to potential language bias?

A. Assuming that ELLs are not capable of high achievement
B. Comparing ELLs' results to native English speakers without adjustments
C. Relying solely on the results to make placement decisions
D. Disregarding any differences in scores between ELLs

Answer:

QUESTION 159

In addition to standardized test scores, what additional sources of information should educators consider when interpreting assessment results for ELLs?

A. Ignoring any additional sources to avoid bias
B. Only considering anecdotal evidence from teachers
C. Including classroom observations, student work samples, and language proficiency assessments
D. Relying solely on parents' opinions about their child's abilities

Answer:

QUESTION 160

What should Samantha do to communicate assessment results effectively?

A. Provide raw scores without any explanations
B. Use technical jargon to impress parents
C. Offer clear explanations of the results and their implications
D. Only communicate positive outcomes to avoid concerns

Answer:

QUESTION 161

What approach should Carlos use to align assessments with standards and address language needs?

A. Design assessments unrelated to the science content
B. Use only multiple-choice questions to assess language skills
C. Consider the language demands of science concepts in his assessments
D. Assess students' language proficiency without considering the content

Answer:

QUESTION 162

What factor should Marta consider when interpreting lower standardized test scores for ELLs compared to English-speaking peers?

A. Assuming that ELLs are not capable of achieving higher scores
B. Disregarding the test scores and focusing solely on classroom performance
C. Recognizing potential language bias in the test and considering language proficiency
D. Blaming the students for not studying enough for the test

Answer:

QUESTION 163

Which legal decision had a significant impact on the education of English Language Learners (ELLs) in the United States?

- A.   Brown v. Board of Education
- B.   Roe v. Wade
- C.   Miranda v. Arizona
- D.   Plessy v. Ferguson

Answer:

QUESTION 164

Which national legislation provides funding for English Language Learners and aims to improve their academic achievement?

- A.   No Child Left Behind Act (NCLB)
- B.   Americans with Disabilities Act (ADA)
- C.   Social Security Act
- D.   Clean Air Act

Answer:

QUESTION 165

How did the Supreme Court decision Lau v. Nichols (1974) impact ESOL programs in the United States?

- A.   It led to the creation of bilingual education programs.
- B.   It established the first ESOL standards for curriculum development.
- C.   It granted citizenship to all English Language Learners.
- D.   It prohibited the enrollment of ELLs in public schools.

Answer:

QUESTION 166

Which strategy is effective for an ESL teacher to set achievable professional goals?

- A.   Setting vague and general goals to allow for flexibility.
- B.   Avoiding timelines to reduce pressure and stress.
- C.   Utilizing the SMART goal-setting framework.
- D.   Relying solely on the school administration to set goals.

Answer:

QUESTION 167

Which opportunity would best support an ESL teacher's professional growth?

- A.   Attending workshops and conferences focused only on ESL teaching techniques.
- B.   Staying within the comfort zone and not seeking new challenges.
- C.   Participating in cross-disciplinary workshops to broaden teaching perspectives.
- D.   Avoiding collaboration with other teachers to maintain individuality.

Answer:

QUESTION 168

Which professional development activity would be most beneficial for an ESL teacher aiming to improve classroom language instruction?

A. Participating in a dance workshop to enhance physical education teaching skills.
B. Attending a language immersion program for personal language learning.
C. Joining a debate club to develop public speaking abilities.
D. Enrolling in a TESOL (Teaching English to Speakers of Other Languages) certification program.

Answer:

QUESTION 169

How can an ESL teacher effectively collaborate with content-area teachers to support English Language Learners' academic success?

A. By discouraging content-area teachers from modifying their lessons for ELLs.
B. By keeping ELLs in separate classes to avoid language barriers.
C. By providing content-area teachers with language support strategies.
D. By avoiding communication with content-area teachers to maintain autonomy.

Answer:

QUESTION 170

What role can technology play in enhancing collaboration between ESL teachers and content-area teachers?

A. Technology may hinder collaboration due to potential communication issues.
B. Technology can facilitate real-time communication through video conferencing.
C. Technology is unnecessary as face-to-face meetings are more effective.
D. Technology is only useful for administrative tasks, not collaboration.

Answer:

QUESTION 171

What approach would best encourage collaboration among ESL teachers and content-area teachers in a school?

A. Assigning teachers to work in isolation to develop their unique teaching methods.
B. Holding regular meetings for teachers of each subject separately to discuss student progress.
C. Establishing interdisciplinary teams that include both ESL and content-area teachers.
D. Relying solely on ESL teachers to provide support for all ELLs in the school.

Answer:

QUESTION 172

As an ESOL resource, how can a teacher support classroom teachers in meeting the needs of English Language Learners?

A. By exclusively focusing on providing direct instruction to ELLs.
B. By offering workshops on content-specific topics to classroom teachers.
C. By avoiding sharing resources and teaching techniques with other teachers.
D. By limiting communication to written memos and emails.

Answer:

QUESTION 173

How can an ESOL resource teacher contribute to the school community beyond the classroom setting?

   A. By focusing solely on individual tutoring for ELLs.
   B. By participating in school-wide committees and professional development activities.
   C. By avoiding collaboration with other teachers to maintain independence.
   D. By refraining from sharing resources or ideas with colleagues.

Answer:

QUESTION 174

How can an ESOL resource teacher effectively communicate with parents of English Language Learners?

   A. By using complex educational jargon to demonstrate expertise.
   B. By sending messages in a language that parents may not understand well.
   C. By organizing parent-teacher conferences with a translator if needed.
   D. By avoiding parent involvement to maintain a professional boundary.

Answer:

QUESTION 175

One of the legal decisions that significantly affected ESOL programs is:

   A. Roe v. Wade
   B. Brown v. Board of Education
   C. Miranda v. Arizona
   D. Plessy v. Ferguson

Answer:

QUESTION 176

Which national legislation specifically addresses funding and support for English Language Learners?

   A. No Child Left Behind Act (NCLB)
   B. Social Security Act
   C. Clean Air Act
   D. Voting Rights Act of 1965

Answer:

QUESTION 177

How did the Supreme Court decision in Lau v. Nichols (1974) impact ESOL programs in the United States?

   A. It granted citizenship to all English Language Learners.
   B. It established the first ESOL standards for curriculum development.
   C. It led to the creation of bilingual education programs.
   D. It prohibited the enrollment of ELLs in public schools.

Answer:

QUESTION 178

Which approach would be most effective for Ms. Jackson to set her professional goals?

 A. Setting broad and unspecific goals to allow for flexibility.
 B. Avoiding setting any professional goals to reduce stress.
 C. Utilizing the SMART goal-setting framework.
 D. Relying solely on her school administration to set goals for her.

Answer:

QUESTION 179

To pursue professional growth opportunities, which action would be most beneficial for Ms. Jackson?

 A. Staying within her comfort zone and avoiding new challenges.
 B. Attending workshops and conferences solely focused on ESL teaching techniques.
 C. Collaborating with teachers from various subject areas in cross-disciplinary workshops.
 D. Avoiding communication with colleagues to maintain individuality.

Answer:

QUESTION 180

Ms. Jackson is considering pursuing additional qualifications to enhance her teaching skills. Which opportunity aligns best with her goal of improving classroom language instruction?

 A. Participating in a dance workshop to enhance her physical education teaching skills.
 B. Attending a language immersion program for personal language learning.
 C. Joining a debate club to develop her public speaking abilities.
 D. Enrolling in a TESOL (Teaching English to Speakers of Other Languages) certification program.

Answer:

QUESTION 181

How can Mr. Lee effectively collaborate with content-area teachers to support English Language Learners' academic success?

 A. By avoiding communication with content-area teachers to maintain autonomy.
 B. By providing content-area teachers with language support strategies.
 C. By asking content-area teachers to modify their lessons for ELLs without his input.
 D. By excluding ELLs from regular classrooms to avoid language barriers.

Answer:

QUESTION 182

Mr. Lee has noticed that some content-area teachers are hesitant to modify their lessons for English Language Learners. What could be a potential strategy for addressing this challenge?

 A. Encouraging content-area teachers to ignore the needs of ELLs and focus on other students.
 B. Organizing a separate classroom exclusively for English Language Learners.
 C. Providing professional development workshops on ELL instructional strategies for content-area teachers.
 D. Requesting that content-area teachers prioritize ELLs' language development over their subject knowledge.

Answer:

QUESTION 183

How can technology facilitate collaboration between Mr. Lee and content-area teachers?

- A. Technology may hinder collaboration due to potential communication issues.
- B. Technology can facilitate real-time communication through video conferencing.
- C. Technology is unnecessary as face-to-face meetings are more effective.
- D. Technology is only useful for administrative tasks, not collaboration.

Answer:

QUESTION 184

How can Mrs. Smith effectively support classroom teachers in meeting the needs of English Language Learners?

- A. By exclusively focusing on providing direct instruction to ELLs.
- B. By offering workshops on content-specific topics to classroom teachers.
- C. By avoiding sharing resources and teaching techniques with other teachers.
- D. By limiting communication to written memos and emails.

Answer:

QUESTION 185

In what ways can Mrs. Smith contribute to the school community beyond the classroom setting?

- A. By focusing solely on individual tutoring for ELLs.
- B. By participating in school-wide committees and professional development activities.
- C. By avoiding collaboration with other teachers to maintain independence.
- D. By refraining from sharing resources or ideas with colleagues.

Answer:

QUESTION 186

How can Mrs. Smith effectively communicate with parents of English Language Learners?

- A. By using complex educational jargon to demonstrate expertise.
- B. By sending messages in a language that parents may not understand well.
- C. By organizing parent-teacher conferences with a translator if needed.
- D. By avoiding parent involvement to maintain a professional boundary.

Answer:

QUESTION 187

Which of the following assessment methods is best suited for evaluating an English Language Learner's understanding of content-area concepts?

- A. True/False test
- B. Multiple-choice test
- C. Performance-based task
- D. Fill-in-the-blank test

Answer:

QUESTION 188

During a classroom assessment, an English Language Learner consistently performs well on oral discussions but struggles with written assessments. What should the teacher consider when interpreting the results?

    A.   The student needs additional help with speaking skills.
    B.   The student might have a language barrier affecting writing abilities.
    C.   The student is not adequately prepared for the assessments.
    D.   The student has a preference for oral communication over written communication.

Answer:

QUESTION 189

Which type of assessment is more suitable for gauging a student's progress over time in content-area learning for English Language Learners?

    A.   Formative assessment
    B.   Summative assessment
    C.   Diagnostic assessment
    D.   Norm-referenced assessment

Answer:

QUESTION 190

Which feature distinguishes content-based instruction from traditional language instruction for English Language Learners?

    A.   Focusing solely on language skills such as grammar and vocabulary.
    B.   Using authentic materials related to content areas.
    C.   Utilizing translation exercises for better comprehension.
    D.   Providing isolated language drills for practice.

Answer:

QUESTION 191

Which of the following is a primary goal of sheltered instruction for English Language Learners in a content classroom?

    A.   Isolating ELLs from their peers to provide personalized attention.
    B.   Teaching only essential vocabulary and grammar to accelerate language acquisition.
    C.   Allowing ELLs to observe content instruction without active participation.
    D.   Making content comprehensible while developing language skills.

Answer:

QUESTION 192

In content-based language instruction, what is the role of language objectives?

    A.   They are separate from content objectives and taught in isolation.
    B.   They are incidental and not explicitly stated.
    C.   They focus on language proficiency levels without considering content.
    D.   They support content learning by highlighting language skills necessary for understanding and expressing knowledge.

Answer:

QUESTION 193

What is one effective instructional strategy for developing academic language proficiency in English Language Learners?

   A. Limiting exposure to complex texts to avoid overwhelming students.
   B. Encouraging the use of simplified language to ensure understanding.
   C. Providing opportunities for authentic language use in meaningful contexts.
   D. Discouraging discussions and group activities to minimize language barriers.

Answer:

QUESTION 194

What is the purpose of using visual aids and graphic organizers in content-area instruction for English Language Learners?

   A. To reduce the amount of language used in the classroom.
   B. To make the classroom environment more visually appealing.
   C. To help ELLs comprehend and organize information effectively.
   D. To replace traditional written assessments with visual assessments.

Answer:

QUESTION 195

Which instructional strategy is most effective for scaffolding content-area tasks for English Language Learners?

   A. Assigning tasks only to students who demonstrate advanced language proficiency.
   B. Providing pre-made answers and solutions to all tasks.
   C. Breaking complex tasks into smaller, manageable steps.
   D. Removing challenging vocabulary and concepts from the tasks.

Answer:

QUESTION 196

What is the primary purpose of using phonics-based activities in teaching beginning reading to English Language Learners (ELLs)?

   A. To develop their conversational fluency.
   B. To enhance their listening skills.
   C. To improve their pronunciation of difficult words.
   D. To help them decode and recognize written words.

Answer:

QUESTION 197

When teaching ELLs to write, why is it important to provide model texts and examples?

   A. To limit their creativity and encourage conformity.
   B. To make the writing process more complex and challenging.
   C. To expose them to different writing styles and structures.
   D. To reduce their engagement with the writing topic.

Answer:

QUESTION 198

How can graphic organizers be beneficial when teaching ELLs beginning writing skills?

    A.   By eliminating the need for students to generate ideas independently.
    B.   By increasing the amount of writing required for each task.
    C.   By hindering students' creativity and self-expression.
    D.   By visually organizing ideas and aiding in the planning process.

Answer:

QUESTION 199

When teaching ELLs to comprehend academic texts, which strategy encourages them to actively engage with the content?

    A.   Summarizing the entire text before reading it.
    B.   Relying solely on background knowledge.
    C.   Annotating and highlighting key points while reading.
    D.   Memorizing the text word-for-word.

Answer:

QUESTION 200

How can pre-teaching vocabulary before reading an academic text benefit ELLs?

    A.   It reduces the need for ELLs to read the entire text.
    B.   It limits their exposure to new words.
    C.   It enhances their understanding of the text's content.
    D.   It discourages critical thinking about unfamiliar words.

Answer:

QUESTION 201

In promoting reading skills for social purposes, what activity can help ELLs develop their ability to infer emotions and intentions in written texts?

    A.   Focusing solely on explicit information.
    B.   Ignoring tone and context.
    C.   Analyzing the author's biography.
    D.   Identifying emotional cues and context clues.

Answer:

QUESTION 202

When teaching ELLs to write for academic purposes, what is the purpose of modeling the process of constructing a well-organized essay?

    A.   To discourage students from seeking outside help.
    B.   To make the writing process more time-consuming.
    C.   To provide a step-by-step guide for effective writing.
    D.   To prevent students from developing their own ideas.

Answer:

QUESTION 203

How can peer feedback contribute to the writing development of ELLs?

- A. By creating an environment of competition and comparison.
- B. By diminishing students' self-confidence in their writing.
- C. By providing diverse perspectives and constructive criticism.
- D. By allowing students to copy each other's work.

Answer:

QUESTION204

What is the benefit of integrating real-world writing tasks, such as composing emails or letters, into ELLs' writing instruction?

- A. It isolates writing from practical communication skills.
- B. It limits students' exposure to different writing formats.
- C. It helps ELLs understand the relevance of writing in daily life.
- D. It restricts writing to academic contexts only.

Answer:

QUESTION 205

Which instructional strategy is most effective for promoting English Language Learners' listening skills?

- A. Providing audio recordings with no accompanying visuals.
- B. Using complex academic lectures beyond their proficiency level.
- C. Engaging in interactive listening activities with visual aids.
- D. Assigning written transcripts without audio support.

Answer:

QUESTION 206

What can be a potential challenge for English Language Learners when developing listening skills?

- A. Exposure to diverse accents and speech rates.
- B. Focusing solely on written transcripts for practice.
- C. Avoiding real-life listening situations.
- D. Limiting listening activities to short dialogues.

Answer:

QUESTION 207

How can an ESL teacher promote active listening skills among English Language Learners?

- A. Encourage note-taking while listening to lectures or audio materials.
- B. Restrict listening activities to audio-only formats.
- C. Avoid using visuals to avoid distractions.
- D. Provide minimal opportunities for student responses during listening tasks.

Answer:

QUESTION 208

Which instructional approach best supports English Language Learners' development of speaking skills?

- A. Providing isolated grammar exercises.
- B. Focusing on memorization of vocabulary lists.
- C. Engaging in authentic and meaningful conversations.
- D. Relying solely on written prompts for speaking practice.

Answer:

QUESTION 209

What is an effective strategy to help English Language Learners build confidence in their speaking abilities?

- A. Correcting every mistake made during speaking tasks.
- B. Encouraging frequent comparison with native speakers.
- C. Providing opportunities for small group discussions.
- D. Limiting speaking practice to scripted dialogues.

Answer:

QUESTION 210

How can an ESL teacher assess the speaking proficiency of English Language Learners?

- A. Conducting multiple-choice tests on speaking topics.
- B. Observing their nonverbal communication during class.
- C. Administering written exams on speaking skills.
- D. Recording and evaluating their oral presentations.

Answer:

QUESTION 211

What is an appropriate method for assessing English Language Learners' reading comprehension?

- A. Relying solely on standardized reading tests.
- B. Using texts that are far above their proficiency level.
- C. Incorporating authentic texts relevant to their interests.
- D. Evaluating reading skills through multiple-choice quizzes.

Answer:

QUESTION 212

What is an essential factor to consider when assessing English Language Learners' reading development?

- A. The use of complicated vocabulary and academic jargon.
- B. The time limit imposed on reading assessments.
- C. Prioritizing grammatical accuracy over comprehension.
- D. Providing opportunities for rereading and reflection.

Answer:

QUESTION 213

Which assessment approach encourages English Language Learners' intrinsic motivation for reading?

- A. Assigning isolated reading passages with no follow-up activities.
- B. Providing extrinsic rewards for completing reading tasks.
- C. Allowing students to choose reading materials aligned with their interests.
- D. Focusing on speed reading exercises.

Answer:

QUESTION 214

What is an effective way to assess English Language Learners' writing development?

- A. Focusing solely on grammatical accuracy.
- B. Providing written feedback without explanations.
- C. Evaluating both content and language proficiency.
- D. Assigning timed writing tasks with no preparation time.

Answer:

QUESTION 215

What is a valuable practice when assessing English Language Learners' writing skills?

- A. Ignoring cultural and linguistic differences in their writing.
- B. Focusing solely on errors and overlooking strengths.
- C. Using rubrics with clear criteria and expectations.
- D. Limiting writing topics to academic subjects only.

Answer:

QUESTION 216

How can an ESL teacher support English Language Learners' writing development?

- A. Providing model essays with identical content for imitation.
- B. Limiting opportunities for peer feedback and collaboration.
- C. Discouraging the use of dictionaries during writing tasks.
- D. Encouraging self-expression and creativity in their writing.

Answer:

QUESTION 217

Which of the following vocabulary instruction strategies is likely to be most effective for English Language Learners (ELLs) in improving their speaking skills?

- A. Providing a list of vocabulary words with their definitions and asking students to memorize them.
- B. Encouraging ELLs to engage in regular conversations with native English speakers outside the classroom.
- C. Using a variety of authentic and context-rich materials to expose ELLs to new vocabulary in meaningful contexts.
- D. Having ELLs write out vocabulary words multiple times to reinforce their understanding.

Answer:

QUESTION 218

Which of the following activities is most likely to enhance English Language Learners' (ELLs) reading and writing development through vocabulary instruction?

A. Asking ELLs to memorize a list of synonyms and antonyms for common words.
B. Encouraging ELLs to engage in peer discussions to explain new vocabulary words.
C. Providing ELLs with a weekly list of unrelated vocabulary words for memorization.
D. Having ELLs complete vocabulary worksheets with matching exercises.

Answer:

QUESTION 219

Which of the following is a research-supported strategy for teaching vocabulary to English Language Learners (ELLs) to enhance their listening skills?

A. Giving ELLs a comprehensive list of advanced vocabulary words to memorize.
B. Using visual aids and real-life objects to illustrate the meaning of new words.
C. Encouraging ELLs to rely solely on translation apps to understand new words.
D. Providing ELLs with complex texts that are beyond their current proficiency level.

Answer:

QUESTION 220

As an ESL teacher, you want to assess your students' oral language development in English. Which of the following assessment methods is likely to be most effective for this purpose?

A. Asking students to write an essay about their favorite topic in English.
B. Administering a multiple-choice test on grammar rules and vocabulary.
C. Conducting one-on-one interviews with students to engage in conversations.
D. Assigning a group project that involves written and spoken components.

Answer:

QUESTION 221

Which of the following assessment approaches is most suitable for evaluating English Language Learners' (ELLs) aural language development in English?

A. Administering a written test that focuses on grammar and sentence structure.
B. Conducting a listening comprehension exercise with multiple-choice questions.
C. Having ELLs participate in a debate or a group discussion.
D. Asking ELLs to write a short story in English.

Answer:

QUESTION 222

You want to assess English Language Learners' (ELLs) progress in their oral language development. Which of the following assessment methods would be most appropriate for measuring long-term progress?

A. Conducting a short role-playing activity with a specific scenario.
B. Observing and recording ELLs' participation in class discussions over the course of a semester.
C. Administering a one-time speaking test with random topics.
D. Assigning ELLs a written report on a topic of their choice.

Answer:

QUESTION 223

Which of the following instructional practices is most effective for promoting English Language Learners' (ELLs) development of listening skills for social purposes?

    A. Providing ELLs with a list of common slang terms used by native speakers.
    B. Encouraging ELLs to watch popular TV shows in English without subtitles.
    C. Engaging ELLs in conversations with native English speakers in a controlled, quiet environment.
    D. Playing audio recordings of authentic social interactions with accompanying transcripts.

Answer:

QUESTION 224

Which of the following strategies is most likely to enhance English Language Learners' (ELLs) listening skills for social purposes?

    A. Encouraging ELLs to avoid watching English movies to focus on language learning.
    B. Providing ELLs with a list of complex idiomatic expressions without context.
    C. Engaging ELLs in role-playing activities that mimic everyday social interactions.
    D. Asking ELLs to read lengthy articles in English to improve their listening comprehension.

Answer:

QUESTION 225

As an ESL teacher, you want to help English Language Learners (ELLs) develop active listening skills for social purposes. What is an effective strategy to achieve this goal?

    A. Encouraging ELLs to listen passively to English radio programs.
    B. Having ELLs transcribe long speeches or lectures without support.
    C. Providing ELLs with opportunities to engage in interactive listening tasks.
    D. Assigning ELLs to complete listening comprehension exercises in silence.

Answer:

QUESTION 226

Which of the following instructional practices is most effective for promoting English Language Learners' (ELLs) development of speaking skills for social purposes?

    A. Providing ELLs with a list of complex idiomatic expressions without context.
    B. Engaging ELLs in regular solo presentations without peer feedback.
    C. Encouraging ELLs to participate in group discussions on relevant topics.
    D. Asking ELLs to write long essays to improve their speaking proficiency

Answer:

QUESTION 227

Which of the following strategies is likely to be most beneficial in helping English Language Learners (ELLs) overcome shyness or speaking anxiety when engaging in social interactions?

    A. Asking ELLs to deliver impromptu speeches in front of the entire class.
    B. Providing ELLs with a supportive and safe environment for practicing speaking.
    C. Encouraging ELLs to speak only in their native language to build confidence.
    D. Giving ELLs negative feedback on their speaking performance.

Answer:

QUESTION 228

To enhance English Language Learners' (ELLs) development of speaking skills for social purposes, what should an ESL teacher prioritize in classroom activities?

    A.   Assigning individual speaking tasks that require lengthy monologues.
    B.   Focusing primarily on grammar correction during speaking practice.
    C.   Providing opportunities for meaningful and interactive pair or group discussions.
    D.   Discouraging ELLs from using visual aids during their presentations.

Answer:

QUESTION 229

What is a key aspect of creating a student-centered learning community for English Language Learners (ELLs)?

    A.   Providing only individual assignments to develop independence.
    B.   Focusing solely on grammar drills and exercises.
    C.   Encouraging collaborative activities and group projects.
    D.   Limiting classroom interactions to teacher-led discussions.

Answer:

QUESTION 230

How can a teacher promote a positive classroom environment for ELLs?

    A.   Assigning only high-stakes, timed assessments.
    B.   Using complex academic language exclusively.
    C.   Incorporating culturally diverse materials and experiences.
    D.   Relying solely on teacher-directed instruction.

Answer:

QUESTION 231

What is the role of the teacher in managing a student-centered learning community for ELLs?

    A.   Dictating rigid classroom rules without flexibility.
    B.   Providing minimal opportunities for student input and choice.
    C.   Adapting instruction to meet diverse learning needs.
    D.   Discouraging student interactions to maintain control.

Answer:

QUESTION 232

What is an effective strategy for providing comprehensible input to ELLs?

    A.   Using complex vocabulary without context.
    B.   Speaking rapidly in the target language.
    C.   Incorporating visuals and gestures to support meaning.
    D.   Avoiding repetition of key concepts.

Answer:

QUESTION 233

How can a teacher promote English language development through interaction?

- A. Minimizing opportunities for student communication.
- B. Focusing solely on written assignments.
- C. Encouraging peer discussions and partner activities.
- D. Exclusively using passive learning materials.

Answer:

QUESTION 234

What is a crucial aspect of providing effective feedback to ELLs?

- A. Giving vague and general comments.
- B. Focusing solely on correcting grammar mistakes.
- C. Providing specific praise and constructive suggestions.
- D. Withholding feedback to encourage self-discovery.

Answer:

QUESTION 235

How can a teacher support the language development of English Language Learners (ELLs) with interrupted formal education (SIFE)?

- A. Providing advanced grade-level materials only.
- B. Tailoring instruction to their individual needs and backgrounds.
- C. Isolating them from their peers to focus on basics.
- D. Ignoring their prior educational experiences.

Answer:

QUESTION 236

What is an effective strategy for supporting the language development of ELLs with special needs?

- A. Excluding them from classroom activities.
- B. Relying solely on written materials.
- C. Implementing differentiated instruction and accommodations.
- D. Avoiding collaboration with special education professionals.

Answer:

QUESTION 237

How can a teacher promote the language development of gifted and talented ELLs?

- A. Providing them with identical tasks as other students.
- B. Offering enrichment opportunities and challenging activities.
- C. Discouraging advanced vocabulary and complex tasks.
- D. Neglecting their academic needs due to language barriers.

Answer:

QUESTION 238

How can a teacher encourage a sense of belonging among English Language Learners (ELLs) in the classroom?

- A. Assigning individual tasks without opportunities for collaboration.
- B. Using only one teaching approach for all ELLs.
- C. Fostering open communication and valuing diverse perspectives.
- D. Avoiding any mention of cultural backgrounds.

Answer:

QUESTION 239

What role does cultural competence play in creating a student-centered learning environment for ELLs?

- A. Ignoring cultural differences to promote uniformity.
- B. Treating all students in the same manner regardless of background.
- C. Acknowledging and respecting diverse cultural backgrounds.
- D. Avoiding any mention of culture to prevent misunderstandings.

Answer:

QUESTION 240

How can a teacher utilize technology to enhance a student-centered learning community for ELLs?

- A. Avoiding technology to prioritize traditional teaching methods.
- B. Providing limited access to technology for certain students.
- C. Integrating technology tools that support language acquisition and collaboration.
- D. Relying solely on technology for instruction without human interaction.

Answer:

QUESTION 241

What is the benefit of incorporating authentic materials into English language instruction?

- A. Limiting exposure to real-life language use.
- B. Focusing only on simplified language materials.
- C. Providing meaningful context and exposure to real-world language.
- D. Using outdated materials for historical accuracy.

Answer:

QUESTION 242

How can a teacher create opportunities for ELLs to use language for real-life purposes?

- A. Restricting language practice to scripted dialogues.
- B. Minimizing opportunities for practical language use.
- C. Integrating authentic tasks, such as role-plays and simulations.
- D. Avoiding any emphasis on practical language skills.

Answer:

QUESTION 243

What is the role of scaffolding in promoting English language development?

- A. Presenting complex tasks without support.
- B. Avoiding any instructional support to promote independence.
- C. Providing temporary support and guidance to help ELLs succeed.
- D. Withholding all support to encourage self-discovery.

Answer:

QUESTION 244

How can a teacher differentiate instruction for English Language Learners (ELLs) with diverse language proficiency levels?

- A. Providing identical tasks for all ELLs regardless of proficiency.
- B. Offering varied tasks and materials based on individual proficiency levels.
- C. Exclusively using advanced academic language for all ELLs.
- D. Ignoring proficiency levels to focus solely on content.

Answer:

QUESTION 245

What is an effective approach for supporting ELLs with limited prior formal education?

- A. Expecting them to quickly catch up to their peers without support.
- B. Providing additional challenges to accelerate their learning.
- C. Implementing targeted interventions and building foundational skills.
- D. Isolating them from the classroom to avoid distractions.

Answer:

QUESTION 246

How can a teacher foster the language development of ELLs with exceptional abilities or talents?

- A. Treating them the same as other students without modifications.
- B. Providing opportunities for enrichment and challenging activities.
- C. Ignoring their talents to avoid creating disparities.
- D. Exclusively focusing on language remediation.

Answer:

QUESTION 247

What is the primary purpose of using icebreaker activities at the beginning of the school year in an ESL classroom?

- A. To assess students' prior language knowledge.
- B. To establish a competitive atmosphere.
- C. To build rapport and create a positive classroom environment.
- D. To introduce complex grammar concepts.

Answer:

QUESTION 248

In a diverse ESL classroom, why is it important to incorporate culturally relevant materials and topics into the curriculum?

    A. To focus solely on the majority culture.
    B. To avoid any potential conflicts.
    C. To enhance students' engagement and cultural awareness.
    D. To limit students' exposure to different perspectives.

Answer:

QUESTION 249

A group of English Language Learners (ELLs) consistently speaks their native language during group activities. What strategy could the teacher implement to encourage more English language use?

    A. Assigning more written assignments to ELLs.
    B. Discouraging group activities altogether.
    C. Providing clear guidelines for using English during group tasks.
    D. Allowing ELLs to use their native language exclusively.

Answer:

QUESTION 250

During a reading activity, an ESL teacher asks students to summarize the main points of a passage in their own words. Which language skill is the teacher primarily targeting?

    A. Listening
    B. Speaking
    C. Reading
    D. Writing

Answer:

QUESTION 251

What is the main purpose of providing comprehensible input in an ESL classroom?

    A. To overwhelm students with complex language structures.
    B. To challenge students with advanced vocabulary.
    C. To ensure that students can understand the language being used.
    D. To discourage students from participating in class discussions.

Answer:

QUESTION 252

An ESL teacher wants to assess students' speaking skills. Which activity would be most effective for this purpose?

    A. Asking students to silently read a passage.
    B. Having students write a short essay.
    C. Engaging students in a role-playing conversation.
    D. Assigning a multiple-choice quiz.

Answer:

QUESTION 253

A new English Language Learner (ELL) has recently arrived in your classroom from a country with interrupted formal education. What initial strategy should you prioritize to support this student's language and academic development?

    A. Placing the student in mainstream classes exclusively.
    B. Providing extra homework assignments for catch-up.
    C. Conducting a language assessment to determine the student's proficiency level.
    D. Enrolling the student in extracurricular activities only.

Answer:

QUESTION 254

How can an ESL teacher best differentiate instruction for a gifted and talented English Language Learner (ELL)?

    A. Providing the same assignments as the rest of the class.
    B. Assigning simpler tasks to prevent overwhelming the student.
    C. Offering more challenging and enriching activities.
    D. Exempting the student from all assessments.

Answer:

QUESTION 255

An English Language Learner (ELL) with special needs struggles with reading comprehension. What approach would be most effective in providing support?

    A. Avoiding reading activities to reduce the student's frustration.
    B. Assigning complex texts to challenge the student.
    C. Providing simplified texts and visual aids, along with targeted reading strategies.
    D. Assigning only writing tasks to strengthen the student's language skills.

Answer:

QUESTION 256

As an ESL teacher, you are introducing a new set of vocabulary words to your English Language Learners (ELLs). Which instructional strategy would be most effective in helping ELLs understand the meanings of these new words?

    A. Providing a list of the words and their definitions for the students to memorize.
    B. Encouraging students to use the new words in sentences during class discussions.
    C. Asking students to look up the definitions of the words in the dictionary on their own.
    D. Assigning a vocabulary quiz at the end of the week to test their knowledge.

Answer:

QUESTION 257

When planning vocabulary instruction for English Language Learners (ELLs), which of the following factors should an ESL teacher consider as a priority?

    A. Incorporating complex academic vocabulary from various subjects.
    B. Focusing on words that are rarely used in everyday conversations.
    C. Teaching vocabulary in isolation without relating it to real-life situations.
    D. Selecting words that have no cognates in the students' native language.

Answer:

QUESTION 258

As an ESL teacher, you notice that some of your English Language Learners (ELLs) are struggling to retain the new vocabulary words taught in the previous week. What would be the most effective approach to address this issue?

A. Repeating the same vocabulary words and definitions during each class session.
B. Asking the students' native language-speaking peers to help them memorize the words.
C. Engaging ELLs in interactive and hands-on activities that use the new vocabulary.
D. Providing ELLs with a written test to assess their understanding of the vocabulary.

Answer:

QUESTION 259

As an ESL teacher, you want to assess your English Language Learners' oral language development in English. Which assessment method would provide the most comprehensive insights into their progress?

A. Administering a written grammar test.
B. Conducting individual speaking interviews with each ELL.
C. Evaluating the students' written essays.
D. Observing the students' participation in group discussions.

Answer:

QUESTION 260

In an ESL classroom, an effective way to assess English Language Learners' aural language development is by:

A. Evaluating their performance in written vocabulary quizzes.
B. Observing their interactions with native English-speaking peers.
C. Giving them reading comprehension tests.
D. Administering listening comprehension activities with questions.

Answer:

QUESTION 261

A teacher is planning to assess English Language Learners' listening skills in a classroom setting. What would be the most appropriate assessment strategy?

A. Having students watch a movie and write a summary of the plot.
B. Playing an audio recording and asking comprehension questions afterward.
C. Assigning a reading passage and evaluating their written responses.
D. Conducting group discussions on various topics.

Answer:

QUESTION262

As an ESL teacher, what instructional approach would best promote English Language Learners' listening skills for informal social purposes, such as everyday conversations?

A. Engaging students in debates and structured discussions.
B. Providing lectures and note-taking activities.
C. Incorporating authentic audio materials with natural language.
D. Assigning reading passages and comprehension questions.

Answer:

QUESTION 263

How can an ESL teacher best encourage English Language Learners to develop active listening skills in the classroom?

- A. Minimizing opportunities for group discussions and activities.
- B. Focusing on rote memorization of vocabulary words.
- C. Providing opportunities for students to ask questions during lectures.
- D. Encouraging students to listen to podcasts and lectures outside of class.

Answer:

QUESTION 264

As an ESL teacher, which activity would be most effective in helping English Language Learners develop their listening skills for academic purposes, such as understanding complex lectures or presentations?

- A. Watching subtitled movies and discussing the plot with peers.
- B. Participating in role-plays and dramatizations.
- C. Listening to audio recordings of academic lectures and taking notes.
- D. Playing listening games and quizzes in pairs.

Answer:

QUESTION 265

Scenario: You have a diverse group of ESL students in your class who come from different cultural backgrounds. During a group activity, one student speaks confidently and dominates the conversation, while another student remains silent and hesitant to participate. How do you address this situation to promote speaking skills and encourage participation?

- A. Assign the silent student a different task that doesn't involve speaking to avoid discomfort.
- B. Praise the confident student and encourage them to lead the conversation continuously.
- C. Ask the confident student to support and involve the silent student by asking them open-ended questions.
- D. Ignore the situation and let the students handle it among themselves.

Answer:

QUESTION 266

Scenario: Your ESL students have shown proficiency in everyday conversations but struggle when it comes to participating in group discussions about academic topics. How can you support their development of speaking skills for academic purposes?

- A. Provide opportunities for students to engage in role-play activities based on real-life scenarios.
- B. Avoid complex academic topics and stick to familiar, everyday subjects during discussions.
- C. Assign reading materials above their current language proficiency level to challenge them.
- D. Encourage students to focus solely on grammar and pronunciation during academic discussions.

Answer:

QUESTION 267

Scenario: Your ESL students are preparing to participate in a debate about environmental issues. Some students have strong opinions and are outspoken, while others are more reserved and find it challenging to express their thoughts clearly. How can you help all students actively contribute to the debate and improve their speaking skills?

- A. Allow the outspoken students to lead the debate while the reserved students take notes.
- B. Divide the class into groups, with each group focusing on a specific environmental issue.
- C. Encourage all students to research and prepare arguments with supporting evidence.
- D. Assign speaking roles based on language proficiency levels, giving the advanced students more speaking time.

Answer:

QUESTION 268

Scenario: In your ESL class, you notice that some students struggle to comprehend complex academic lectures delivered in English. What can you do to enhance their listening skills and improve understanding?

    A. Provide the students with transcripts of the lectures in their native language for easier comprehension.
    B. Simplify the academic lectures and use basic vocabulary to make it easier for the students to understand.
    C. Encourage students to focus solely on individual words and phrases rather than the overall context.
    D. Use authentic academic materials and gradually scaffold their listening tasks to match their proficiency level.

Answer:

QUESTION 269

Scenario: Your ESL students are preparing for a standardized English listening test, and some of them express anxiety about their listening abilities. How can you help them develop effective strategies for better performance on the test?

    A. Advise them to focus solely on answering the questions correctly without worrying about the listening context.
    B. Encourage them to memorize possible answers to common listening test questions.
    C. Provide practice listening tests that mirror the format of the standardized test.
    D. Advise them to skip the listening section of the test if they find it challenging.

Answer:

QUESTION 270

Scenario: In your ESL class, you have students with varying listening proficiency levels. How can you differentiate your listening instruction to meet the needs of all students?

    A. Assign the same listening tasks to all students to maintain consistency.
    B. Use only visual aids and written materials to support the listening activities.
    C. Provide listening tasks based on students' proficiency levels, adjusting the difficulty accordingly.
    D. Focus solely on grammar exercises to reinforce listening skills.

Answer:

QUESTION 271

Scenario: In your ESL class, you have a mix of confident and shy students who need to present their research projects to the class. How can you create a supportive environment for all students to develop their speaking skills during presentations?

    A. Allow confident students to present without feedback to save time and avoid potential embarrassment.
    B. Ask shy students to provide written reports instead of oral presentations.
    C. Provide clear guidelines and criteria for presentations and encourage peer feedback.
    D. Select only the top-performing students to present, as they are more likely to excel.

Answer:

QUESTION 272

Scenario: Your ESL students need to participate in debates about historical events and their impact on society. Some students are struggling to present well-organized arguments. How can you support their development of speaking skills for academic purposes during debates?

    A. Assign research topics based on students' preferences to ensure they are invested in the debate.
    B. Encourage students to memorize pre-written arguments to avoid improvisation.
    C. Provide guidance on organizing arguments, using evidence, and engaging with opposing viewpoints.
    D. Allow students to rely solely on their personal opinions during the debate.

Answer:

QUESTION 273

Scenario: Your ESL students are preparing to deliver presentations on various cultural traditions and customs. How can you encourage them to develop engaging presentations that effectively convey the information to their audience?

   A.   Limit the students to use text-only slides in their presentations to avoid distractions.
   B.   Encourage students to incorporate multimedia elements and interactive activities in their presentations.
   C.   Assign specific presentation topics to each student without considering their interests.
   D.   Ask students to focus solely on providing facts and data, avoiding personal anecdotes.

Answer:

QUESTION 274

Scenario: In your ESL class, you are assessing your students' reading comprehension skills through a written assessment. Some students perform well in class discussions but struggle to demonstrate their understanding in writing. What can you do to support these students and assess their reading development accurately?

   A.   Assign lower grades to students who perform poorly in written assessments to motivate them to improve.
   B.   Offer extra credit assignments to compensate for low scores in written assessments.
   C.   Provide opportunities for students to discuss their reading responses orally or through group discussions.
   D.   Give the struggling students extra time to complete the written assessment.

Answer:

QUESTION 275

Scenario: Your ESL students come from diverse language backgrounds, and some of them struggle with specific vocabulary and idiomatic expressions while reading in English. How can you assess their reading development more effectively to identify areas of improvement?

   A.   Provide the students with dictionaries during reading assessments to look up unfamiliar words.
   B.   Use only short and straightforward texts to avoid challenging students with unfamiliar language.
   C.   Include questions in the assessment that focus solely on grammar and sentence structure.
   D.   Offer a variety of reading materials that reflect different cultural backgrounds and linguistic levels.

Answer:

QUESTION 276

Scenario: Some ESL students in your class show improvement in reading comprehension during in-class activities but struggle to replicate the same progress in standardized reading tests. How can you address this discrepancy and assess their reading development more accurately?

   A.   Advise the students to practice reading more challenging materials to prepare for standardized tests.
   B.   Disregard the standardized test results as they may not accurately reflect the students' reading abilities.
   C.   Provide additional support and practice with sample questions similar to the ones on the standardized test.
   D.   Focus solely on vocabulary and grammar exercises to enhance reading comprehension skills.

Answer:

QUESTION 277

Maria is an ESL teacher working with a group of English Language Learners. She wants to assess their writing skills. She decides to use a holistic scoring rubric. Which of the following best explains why Maria might choose this approach?

   A.   To provide specific feedback on individual aspects of writing.
   B.   To assign separate scores for content, grammar, and vocabulary.
   C.   To evaluate overall writing quality based on an overall impression.
   D.   To identify specific areas of improvement for each student.

Answer:

QUESTION 278

Jamal, an ESL teacher, is working with young English Language Learners who are at the beginning stages of reading and writing. He wants to promote their phonemic awareness. Which activity would be most effective for achieving this goal?

A. Having students write short paragraphs about their weekends.
B. Reading aloud complex texts and discussing their themes.
C. Playing rhyming games and identifying initial sounds in words.
D. Assigning long reading passages for homework.

Answer:

QUESTION 279

In a diverse classroom, an ESL teacher is aiming to enhance English Language Learners' reading skills for both social and academic purposes. Which instructional strategy would best address this goal?

A. Focusing solely on vocabulary and grammar exercises.
B. Providing opportunities for collaborative group reading and discussions.
C. Assigning lengthy reading passages without any follow-up activities.
D. Emphasizing individual silent reading without any interaction.

Answer:

QUESTION 280

An ESL teacher is working with intermediate English Language Learners and wants to help them develop writing skills for various purposes. Which activity would best serve this goal?

A. Assigning repetitive grammar exercises focused on verb tenses.
B. Providing prompts for creative writing and encouraging imaginative expression.
C. Limiting writing practice to copying sentences from a textbook.
D. Asking students to read complex texts without any writing tasks.

Answer:

QUESTION 281

Jennifer, an ESL teacher, wants to assess her students' writing progress over time. She decides to use formative assessment. Which of the following is the primary purpose of formative assessment in this context?

A. Assigning grades to students' writing assignments.
B. Providing a final evaluation of students' writing skills.
C. Monitoring students' progress and guiding instructional decisions.
D. Comparing students' writing abilities with those of their peers.

Answer:

QUESTION282

Carla, an ESL teacher, is working with young English Language Learners who have limited exposure to English. She wants to build their vocabulary and reading comprehension. Which strategy would be most effective for achieving this goal?

A. Having students listen to complex audiobooks in English.
B. Using picture books and labeling objects in the classroom.
C. Giving students advanced reading materials to challenge them.
D. Assigning lengthy reading passages for homework.

Answer:

QUESTION 283

An ESL teacher is working with a group of English Language Learners who come from diverse cultural backgrounds. To promote their reading skills for a variety of purposes, which strategy would be most effective?

    A. Focusing solely on readings from the teacher's cultural background.
    B. Providing a mix of texts representing various cultures and perspectives.
    C. Assigning texts with complex vocabulary beyond students' levels.
    D. Restricting reading materials to a single genre.

Answer:

QUESTION 284

As an ESL teacher, you have been conducting classroom-based assessments to monitor the content-area learning and concept development of your English Language Learners (ELLs). During the assessment, one of your ELL students consistently performs poorly in written tasks but excels in oral discussions. What should be your immediate course of action?

    A. Focus solely on written tasks to improve the student's writing skills.
    B. Provide extra oral discussion opportunities and ignore the written tasks.
    C. Modify the assessment format to include more oral components.
    D. Utilize various assessment methods to capture the student's strengths and weaknesses accurately.

Answer:

QUESTION285

You are an ESL teacher in a diverse classroom with English Language Learners from various linguistic backgrounds. How can you effectively implement a sheltered instruction approach to cater to the needs of these students while teaching content subjects like science or social studies?

    A. Simplify the content and avoid using realia to prevent confusion.
    B. Incorporate students' native languages as the primary medium of instruction.
    C. Use visual aids, hands-on activities, and clear explanations to make the content accessible.
    D. Limit the use of vocabulary to only basic English words to avoid overwhelming the students.

Answer:

QUESTION 286

You have a group of intermediate level English Language Learners who are studying a unit on historical events in your social studies class. They struggle to grasp the complex academic language and content-area concepts. What can you do to support their comprehension effectively?

    A. Provide pre-made notes and summaries to replace reading the content.
    B. Simplify the vocabulary and content to match their current language level.
    C. Incorporate real-world examples and relevant materials to contextualize the content.
    D. Assign advanced research projects to encourage independent learning.

Answer:

QUESTION 287

You have recently introduced a new content unit to your English Language Learners (ELLs) that involves complex concepts. After several lessons, you notice that some students are struggling to grasp the key ideas. What would be the most appropriate form of assessment to identify their specific areas of difficulty?

    A. Conduct a multiple-choice test to assess their understanding.
    B. Assign a group project to gauge their collaboration skills.
    C. Use formative assessment techniques like classroom discussions and quizzes.
    D. Offer individualized one-on-one tutoring sessions for each student.

Answer:

QUESTION 288

You are planning a content-based ESOL lesson for a group of intermediate-level English Language Learners studying literature. How can you effectively integrate language and content instruction during this lesson?

  A. Assign the students to read the literature independently and discuss their thoughts afterward.
  B. Have the students engage in role-playing activities to practice conversational skills.
  C. Incorporate vocabulary and language exercises related to the literature content.
  D. Provide grammar lessons separately to ensure language proficiency.

Answer:

QUESTION 289

You have a group of English Language Learners who are newcomers and have limited English proficiency. They need to understand a challenging science unit. What instructional strategy can you employ to make the content comprehensible for them?

  A. Provide them with advanced reading materials and encourage independent study.
  B. Use visuals, realia, and hands-on activities to support their understanding.
  C. Assign them to complete written summaries of the science concepts.
  D. Organize a debate on the scientific topics to encourage critical thinking.

Answer:

QUESTION 290

You have a group of English Language Learners who need to develop their critical-thinking skills in the context of social studies. What instructional strategy can you use to promote their critical-thinking abilities effectively?

  A. Assign simple, factual questions for them to answer.
  B. Provide them with a detailed study guide to memorize the content.
  C. Engage them in thought-provoking discussions and debates.
  D. Instruct them to follow a step-by-step process to solve problems.

Answer:

QUESTION 291

You have a diverse group of English Language Learners who are at different proficiency levels. How can you promote their development of important learning skills and strategies effectively to support content-area learning?

  A. Group students solely based on their language proficiency levels.
  B. Assign separate, easier tasks for students with lower language proficiency.
  C. Implement differentiated instruction tailored to individual learning needs.
  D. Encourage students to work independently to develop self-learning skills.

Answer:

This page is intentionally left blank.

Chapter 2 – Answers and Explanations

QUESTION 1

Answer: B

Explanation: Phonemes are the distinct sound units in a language that can change the meaning of a word. In the word "school," the substitution of the /sk/ phoneme with /ʃ/ (as in "sh") can lead to a mispronunciation. Understanding phonemes is crucial for helping ESOL learners produce accurate sounds and words.

QUESTION 2

Answer: B

Explanation: Inflectional morphemes, like "-ed" for past tense, alter the grammatical function of a word without changing its core meaning. Irregular verbs, however, don't always follow the regular pattern. The student's use of "-ed" with irregular verbs indicates a need for understanding the exceptions to this rule.

QUESTION 3

Answer: A

Explanation: Subject-verb agreement refers to the correct pairing of the subject's number (singular or plural) with the appropriate verb form. In the sentence, "She am happy," there is a disagreement between the singular subject "She" and the incorrect verb form "am." The student should use "is" instead of "am" to match the subject's form. Understanding subject-verb agreement is important for constructing grammatically accurate sentences.

QUESTION 4

Answer: B

Explanation: Minimal pairs are pairs of words that differ in only one phoneme and have distinct meanings. In this case, the /θ/ and /s/ sounds create a minimal pair, as they differentiate words like "think" and "sink." Recognizing and practicing minimal pairs can help ESOL learners improve their pronunciation.

QUESTION 5

Answer: C

Explanation: Suprasegmentals refer to aspects of speech that extend beyond individual phonemes, such as intonation, stress, and rhythm. Teaching the correct placement of stress on syllables is essential for conveying proper word and sentence patterns, which aids in effective communication.

QUESTION 6

Answer: A

Explanation: /p/ and /b/ are examples of a voiced-unvoiced pair, where /p/ is unvoiced (no vibration of vocal cords) and /b/ is voiced (vocal cords vibrate). Focusing on the distinct articulatory features, such as tongue placement and lip vibration, helps students grasp the phonemic differences and produce the sounds accurately.

QUESTION 7

Answer: B

Explanation: Sociocultural factors, such as cultural norms and communication styles, can greatly influence language behavior. The student's hesitancy and avoidance of eye contact might stem from cultural differences in communication norms, impacting their language participation and development.

QUESTION 8

Answer: D

Explanation: Frequent relocations and academic disruptions can lead to gaps in vocabulary and content knowledge. Language acquisition is closely tied to academic development, and students with gaps may struggle to comprehend and express complex ideas in their L2 due to limited background knowledge.

QUESTION 9

Answer: D

Explanation: Sociopolitical factors, such as students' professional backgrounds, can shape the specific language demands they encounter. Healthcare professionals may need medical terminology, engineers may require technical vocabulary, and businesspeople might focus on business communication. Recognizing these differences helps tailor instruction to their unique language-learning needs.

QUESTION 10

Answer: B

Explanation: Metacognitive strategies involve self-awareness, self-monitoring, and self-regulation of the learning process. The student's note-taking, study groups, reflection, and adjustment of learning approaches indicate a metacognitive approach to language acquisition.

QUESTION 11

Answer: A

Explanation: Cognitive strategies involve mental processes used to manipulate language materials, such as memory aids. Associating new words with images and personal experiences is a cognitive strategy that enhances memory and vocabulary retention.

QUESTION 12

Answer: C

Explanation: Social/communicative strategies involve interacting with others to improve language skills through negotiation of meaning and contextually relevant communication. The role-play activity engages students in authentic language use and promotes interactive learning.

QUESTION 13

Answer: C

Explanation: Cultural hierarchy refers to the perception of one culture or language as superior to another. Students who are proficient in their native language might feel their skills are devalued in the new context, leading to challenges in accepting and developing their L2 skills.

QUESTION 14

Answer: D

Explanation: Exposure to multiple languages can enhance cognitive flexibility and metalinguistic skills. Students from bilingual households often have experience switching between languages, leading to heightened awareness of language structure and usage.

QUESTION 15

Answer: C

Explanation: Trauma can have significant effects on cognitive and emotional functioning, which in turn can influence language acquisition. Students dealing with trauma may struggle with attention, memory, and emotional regulation, all of which can impact their ability to acquire and develop L2 skills.

QUESTION 16

Answer: B

Explanation: Reading and analyzing authentic texts from various genres allows ESL students to understand the specific features and language structures used in different types of writing. It helps them grasp the conventions of each genre and apply this knowledge to their own writing. This approach enhances critical thinking as students learn to recognize the unique characteristics of each discourse type.

QUESTION 17

Answer: C

Explanation: Encouraging collaborative discussions and debates among ESL students helps improve their oral communication skills. Engaging in meaningful conversations on relevant topics fosters critical thinking, active participation, and the ability to articulate thoughts and opinions effectively. It also allows students to learn from each other, gain confidence, and practice various discourse strategies.

QUESTION 18

Answer: B

Explanation: Addressing pragmatics issues, such as interrupting others, requires explicit instruction and corrective feedback. ESL teachers should help the student understand the social norms and conventions of turn-taking in conversations. By providing guidance and practice, the student can develop appropriate communication skills, enhancing their ability to engage in effective and respectful interactions.

QUESTION 19

Answer: B

Explanation: ESL students need to be familiar with formal registers, such as technical jargon, used in academic and professional settings. Understanding industry-specific language and terms is essential for success in academic studies and specialized careers. Teaching students about formal registers equips them with the language skills needed for more formal and specialized contexts, encouraging critical thinking as they navigate complex topics within these domains.

QUESTION 20

Answer: C

Explanation: By guiding students to identify the main points and supporting details in a text, they can create their own summaries. This approach enhances their critical thinking skills, as they must discern essential information from non-essential details. It also helps improve their understanding of text structure and cohesion, leading to more accurate and effective summarization.

QUESTION 21

Answer: C

Explanation: Facilitating debates on controversial topics encourages ESL students to think critically, analyze information, and form well-reasoned arguments. It requires them to provide evidence and justifications for their opinions, fostering deeper engagement with the subject matter and enhancing their ability to express ideas persuasively.

QUESTION 22

Answer: B

Explanation: For beginner-level students, providing sentence stems and writing templates helps scaffold their writing process. It enables them to focus on organizing ideas and using appropriate language without feeling overwhelmed. By offering a structured framework, students can build their confidence and gradually develop their writing skills, eventually leading to more independent and critical writing.

QUESTION 23

Answer: C

Explanation: Exposing ESL students to authentic conversations allows them to observe how implied meanings are used in context. By discussing the context and the intended messages, students develop their pragmatic understanding and critical thinking skills, enabling them to interpret implied meanings more accurately in various communication situations.

QUESTION 24

Answer: B

Explanation: Addressing the issue of excessive apologies requires explicit instruction on the appropriate use of speech acts. ESL teachers should help students understand when apologies are necessary and when they might be considered excessive. This approach fosters critical thinking as students learn to navigate cultural and situational norms in language use, leading to more effective and contextually appropriate communication.

QUESTION 25

Answer: C

Explanation: Role-playing activities allow ESL students to practice using conversational implicatures and indirect speech acts in simulated real-life scenarios. This practical application of language helps students develop their pragmatic skills, critical thinking, and the ability to infer meaning beyond literal expressions. It also enhances their communication strategies for different social contexts.

QUESTION 26

Answer: C

Explanation: Introducing ESL students to different English language variations and registers helps them adapt their language use to diverse social and professional environments. It allows them to understand the appropriate language for various situations, fostering critical thinking as they navigate different communication norms. This knowledge is crucial for effective communication and success in various contexts.

QUESTION 27

Answer: C

Explanation: Dialects are regional variations of a language that have distinct pronunciation, vocabulary, and grammar. They are equally valid forms of communication and should not be stigmatized or considered incorrect. ESL teachers should recognize the diversity of English dialects and promote understanding and acceptance of different linguistic backgrounds.

QUESTION 28

Answer: D

Explanation: Starting with the formal register allows ESL students to understand the most structured and polite form of communication. As they become comfortable with the formal register, introducing the neutral register helps them grasp a more general and widely used form of language. Finally, exploring the casual register provides insight into informal communication, allowing students to adapt their language use based on social contexts and fostering critical thinking in language variation.

QUESTION 29

Answer: C

Explanation: Supporting L2 literacy development requires explicit instruction on reading strategies that can be transferred from the students' L1 to English. By recognizing the similarities and differences between reading in both languages, students can apply existing reading skills in their native language to comprehend English texts more effectively. This approach encourages critical thinking as students analyze and adapt their strategies, leading to improved reading comprehension in English.

QUESTION 30

Answer: C

Explanation: L1 literacy serves as a valuable resource for ESL students when learning to read and write in English. The cognitive skills and knowledge gained through literacy in their native language can transfer to the L2, supporting their understanding of language structures, reading comprehension, and writing abilities. Recognizing the role of L1 literacy encourages critical thinking as ESL teachers leverage this prior knowledge to enhance L2 literacy development.

QUESTION 31

Answer: B

Explanation: Learning the English alphabet and basic phonics can be challenging for ESL students, especially those who come from languages with different writing systems or phonetic structures. These early literacy skills are fundamental for reading and writing in English. By understanding these challenges, ESL teachers can design appropriate activities and provide targeted support to foster critical thinking and successful literacy development in English.

QUESTION 32

Answer: C

Explanation: Differentiating instruction is crucial in a mixed-level ESL class to meet the diverse needs of students. Tailoring instruction to target each group's proficiency level allows the teacher to provide appropriate materials, tasks, and language support for effective learning. This approach encourages critical thinking as students engage with content that matches their language abilities, fostering growth and progress across proficiency levels.

QUESTION 33

Answer: B

Explanation: Intermediate English language learners typically show proficiency in basic social interactions and everyday conversations. However, they may struggle with abstract or complex topics, which require higher levels of language proficiency. Recognizing these characteristics helps ESL teachers tailor instruction and design activities that gradually challenge students to engage with more complex language and foster critical thinking in various communicative contexts.

QUESTION 34

Answer: D

Explanation: Social-language development primarily focuses on developing conversational and communication skills for everyday interactions, which mainly involve listening and speaking. In contrast, academic-language development includes reading and writing skills necessary for success in educational settings. ESL teachers should consider this difference to design appropriate activities and foster critical thinking across various language domains for both social and academic contexts.

QUESTION 35

Answer: C

Explanation: By encouraging peer collaboration and discussions among ESL students from diverse linguistic backgrounds, they can learn from each other's experiences and share insights about literacy development in their respective languages. This approach fosters critical thinking and cross-linguistic awareness, allowing students to draw connections between their L1 and L2 literacy skills, leading to enhanced L2 literacy development.

QUESTION 36

Answer: C

Explanation: Explicitly teaching reading comprehension strategies, such as identifying key information and making inferences, helps ESL students develop critical thinking skills when approaching complex texts. These strategies are transferable across languages and assist students in comprehending texts in their L2 by focusing on essential details and drawing conclusions. Translating the text into their L1 might provide a temporary solution, but teaching comprehension strategies enhances long-term L2 literacy development.

QUESTION 37

Answer: D

Explanation: Significant differences in grammar and syntax between the students' L1 and English can create challenges in transferring L1 literacy skills to L2 literacy development. These differences might affect the organization and structure of written texts, causing difficulties in understanding and producing English texts. Understanding these linguistic differences helps ESL teachers design targeted instruction to address specific areas of challenge and promote critical thinking in bridging the gap between L1 and L2 literacy skills.

QUESTION 38

Answer: C

Explanation: Inclusive classroom discussions can be fostered by providing opportunities for all students, regardless of proficiency levels, to contribute. ESL teachers should use varying levels of linguistic support, such as sentence starters, visuals, or scaffolding, to ensure that beginning students can participate meaningfully alongside more advanced peers. Encouraging all students to share their ideas promotes critical thinking, respect for diverse perspectives, and language development across proficiency levels.

QUESTION39

Answer: C

Explanation: Beginning English language learners typically demonstrate fluency in everyday conversations and can express basic needs and preferences. However, they may encounter challenges with more complex academic language and may require support when engaging with academic texts. Recognizing these characteristics allows ESL teachers to scaffold instruction appropriately, encouraging critical thinking and language development as students progress to higher proficiency levels.

QUESTION 40

Answer: C

Explanation: Integrating academic language instruction into content-based lessons and assignments helps intermediate-level students develop the language skills needed for academic success. By using academic language in meaningful contexts, students engage in critical thinking and apply language skills relevant to their studies. This approach supports their overall language proficiency and fosters language development within an academic context, preparing them for more advanced language proficiency levels.

QUESTION 41

Answer: C

Explanation: Research suggests that knowledge of the first language (L1) can positively influence the acquisition of a second language (L2). Learners can transfer certain language skills, such as grammar rules and vocabulary, from their native language to the target language, making the learning process smoother.

QUESTION 42

Answer: B

Explanation: Trilingualism refers to the ability of an individual to speak three languages fluently. Bilingualism refers to speaking two languages, while multilingualism is a more general term that encompasses proficiency in multiple languages.

QUESTION 43

Answer: C

Explanation: Heritage language learning refers to the process of learning and maintaining a language that is part of an individual's cultural or familial heritage but is not commonly used in their current community. It often involves maintaining connections with one's cultural identity and linguistic roots.

QUESTION 44

Answer: C

Explanation: Literacy skills developed in the first language (L1) can transfer and support the development of similar skills in the second language (L2). Understanding the structures and functions of reading and writing in L1 can provide a solid foundation for acquiring similar skills in L2.

QUESTION 45

Answer: B

Explanation: Limited access to reading materials and resources in the native language can hinder the development of literacy skills in English language learners. Having access to a variety of reading materials in their native language can support their literacy development and potentially transfer to English literacy skills.

QUESTION 46

Answer: D

Explanation: Syntax is one of the major concepts related to literacy development. It refers to the structure and arrangement of words in sentences and is crucial for understanding grammar and sentence formation in both reading and writing.

QUESTION 47

Answer: C

Explanation: Beginning English language learners (ELLs) often have limited proficiency in English and may rely on nonverbal communication, gestures, and simple vocabulary to express their ideas and needs.

QUESTION 48

Answer: D

Explanation: Basic Interpersonal Communication Skills (BICS) refer to the social language skills used in everyday interactions and casual conversations. These language skills are typically developed faster than academic language skills.

QUESTION 49

Answer: A

Explanation: Intermediate English language learners (ELLs) have developed more advanced language skills and are capable of understanding and using more complex language, including academic vocabulary and structures. They are likely to be able to engage in academic tasks such as reading academic texts and writing essays.

QUESTION 50

Answer: C

Explanation: Instead of correcting or suppressing the students' use of regional dialects, Maria can use this situation as a teaching moment. She can explain to the students and the class as a whole the concept of language variations, including dialects, and how language can differ based on geographical regions or social contexts. This approach promotes a culturally inclusive and supportive learning environment.

QUESTION 51

Answer: C

Explanation: It is essential for the ESL teacher to address the issue of using informal language and slang in academic settings. Instead of embarrassing the student, the teacher can provide explicit instruction on the appropriate use of informal language and explain the differences between informal and formal registers. This guidance will help the student understand the context in which informal language is suitable and when to switch to more formal language in academic settings.

QUESTION 52

Answer: C

Explanation: To engage all students with varying language proficiency levels, the teacher should use authentic materials that represent real-life situations and different registers. This approach exposes learners to a variety of language styles and contexts, making the lesson relevant and applicable to their everyday interactions. It also helps students understand the importance of using appropriate language registers based on different social settings and contexts.

QUESTION 53

Answer: C

Explanation: To help Juan improve his English pronunciation, the teacher should provide targeted practice and drills, including minimal pair exercises. These exercises focus on distinguishing sounds that are similar in both the native and target languages. By practicing these sounds, Juan can become more aware of the differences and improve his pronunciation, making his spoken English more understandable to others.

QUESTION 54

Answer: C

Explanation: To support students with weaker L1 literacy skills, Sofia should provide scaffolding and support during reading and writing tasks. This may include using graphic organizers, vocabulary aids, and other strategies to help students comprehend and express their ideas in English. It is essential to provide targeted support while encouraging the development of English literacy skills without excluding the students from the regular class activities.

QUESTION 55

Answer: C

Explanation: For advanced adult learners, integrating authentic materials and real-world tasks is essential to promote practical language use and cater to their specific needs. This approach allows learners to engage with language in real-life contexts, improving their communication skills beyond the academic setting. It also enhances their ability to understand and use idiomatic expressions, informal language, and language variations commonly encountered in everyday interactions.

QUESTION 56

Answer: C

Explanation: This situation provides an excellent opportunity for the teacher to discuss the concept of language variations and registers with the whole class. Instead of immediately correcting the student or excluding them from the discussion, fostering understanding and acceptance of language diversity will create a more inclusive and respectful learning environment.

QUESTION 57

Answer: C

Explanation: Providing explicit instruction on the appropriate use of language registers is essential in helping the student understand when and where formal language is necessary. It allows the student to develop the ability to switch between informal and formal language, improving their communication skills in various contexts.

QUESTION 58

Answer: C

Explanation: Incorporating authentic materials that showcase diverse language variations allows learners to experience language in real-life contexts. It makes the lesson relevant and engaging for all students, regardless of their cultural backgrounds and proficiency levels. Authentic materials expose learners to different language registers and dialects, enriching their language learning experience.

QUESTION 59

Answer: C

Explanation: Providing targeted language feedback and explaining the differences between Anna's native language and English can help her understand the grammatical structures and make appropriate adjustments. This approach supports Anna's language development without discouraging her from using her native language and creates a positive and supportive learning environment.

QUESTION 60

Answer: C

Explanation: Utilizing students' L1 knowledge can be valuable in making connections and facilitating L2 learning. It allows students to draw upon their existing language skills to understand new concepts and language structures in English. Creating a supportive environment that acknowledges the value of their native language can enhance their language acquisition process.

QUESTION 61

Answer: C

Explanation: To effectively meet the needs of diverse language proficiency levels, the teacher should differentiate instruction by using various language resources and tasks. This approach allows each student to engage with materials and activities that match their language level, fostering individual growth and progress in language acquisition. It encourages a supportive and inclusive learning environment for all learners.

QUESTION 62

Answer: B

Explanation: Phonemes are the distinct units of sound in a language that can change the meaning of words. Morphemes refer to the smallest units of meaning, while syntax deals with sentence structure, and semantics relates to word meanings.

QUESTION 63

Answer: C

Explanation: Language acquisition refers to the innate ability of humans to learn a language without formal instruction. Code-switching involves alternating between languages, bilingualism refers to being proficient in two languages, and linguistic relativity is the idea that language influences thought.

QUESTION 64

Answer: C

Explanation: Syntax refers to the rules that determine how words are organized in a sentence to convey meaning. Phonology deals with the sound system, pragmatics involves language use in context, and morphology is the study of word structure.

QUESTION 65

Answer: C

Explanation: Overgeneralization occurs when a child applies a grammatical rule too broadly, leading to errors like "goed" instead of the correct past tense "went." Underextension is when a word is used in a very limited context, and assimilation is a concept related to phonetics.

QUESTION 66

Answer: C

Explanation: Sociolinguistics examines how language is influenced by social factors, such as culture, region, and social status. Semiotics studies signs and symbols, pragmatics focuses on language use in context, and psycholinguistics explores the psychological processes of language.

QUESTION 67

Answer: B

Explanation: Based on Maria's limited ability to communicate and her use of basic phrases, she falls into the beginning level of English language proficiency.

QUESTION 68

Answer: B

Explanation: Ahmed's ability to engage in discussions and express opinions suggests an intermediate level of English language proficiency, where learners can handle more complex communication tasks.

QUESTION 69

Answer: D

Explanation: Elena's ability to handle both academic and social contexts in English, along with her advanced communication skills, indicates a high level of English language proficiency.

QUESTION 70

Answer: D

Explanation: Carlos's limited exposure to his native language's speakers and unfamiliarity with its use may affect his overall language acquisition and development in his new environment.

QUESTION 71

Answer: D

Explanation: Sociopolitical factors, such as discrimination and anxiety, can create a negative affective filter that hinders language acquisition by blocking information processing and reducing the learner's openness to new language input.

QUESTION 72

Answer: C

Explanation: Raj's strong academic motivation can drive him to engage more deeply with the language and seek out opportunities for learning, ultimately enhancing his language acquisition and development.

QUESTION 73

Answer: A

Explanation: Lila's use of flashcards and language exposure activities falls under cognitive strategies, which involve direct engagement with language materials to improve understanding and recall.

QUESTION 74

Answer: B

Explanation: Javier's reflection, goal-setting, and self-regulation align with metacognitive strategies, which involve planning, monitoring, and evaluating one's learning process.

QUESTION 75

Answer: C

Explanation: Anna's emphasis on group activities, communication, and interaction with others falls under social/communicative strategies, which involve using language in social contexts to improve proficiency.

QUESTION 76

Answer: C

Explanation: The native language spoken by the learner plays a crucial role in L2 acquisition. The similarities and differences between the native language and the target language can influence the ease or difficulty of learning the L2. It can affect pronunciation, grammar, vocabulary, and overall language comprehension.

QUESTION 77

Answer: C

Explanation: Language practice is essential for L2 development. Without sufficient opportunities to use the target language in real-life situations, students may struggle to apply their knowledge effectively. Regular and meaningful language practice is crucial for improving fluency and proficiency in the L2.

QUESTION 78

Answer: B

Explanation: Educational programs that support bilingualism and multiculturalism create an environment where students are encouraged to learn and use multiple languages. This fosters a positive attitude towards language learning and helps students appreciate and value linguistic diversity. Such programs can enhance L2 acquisition by providing a supportive and inclusive learning environment.

QUESTION 79

Answer: C

Explanation: Metacognitive self-assessment involves the learner's ability to reflect on their language learning process, identify their strengths and weaknesses, and make adjustments accordingly. It is a crucial strategy for developing self-awareness and becoming a more effective language learner.

QUESTION 80

Answer: A

Explanation: Mnemonic devices are memory aids that help learners create associations between new words and familiar concepts or images. By forming these mental connections, learners can recall vocabulary more easily, which aids in L2 acquisition.

QUESTION 81

Answer: B

Explanation: Language exchange programs involve interacting with native speakers or proficient speakers of the target language. This strategy provides learners with authentic language practice and the opportunity to engage in real-life conversations, improving fluency and communicative competence in the L2.

QUESTION 82

Answer: C

Explanation: Providing explicit instruction on tongue placement and airflow for the /l/ and /r/ sounds can help students understand the physical differences between the two sounds. It will enable them to make the necessary adjustments in their articulation and improve their pronunciation. This approach addresses the specific phonological issue and supports the students' overall phonological development.

QUESTION 83

Answer: D

Explanation: Explicit instruction on tongue placement and airflow for the /θ/ and /ð/ sounds is essential for students to grasp the correct pronunciation. Practicing these sounds in context, such as using them in sentences and meaningful conversations, helps students internalize the sounds and use them more naturally in their speech. This approach fosters effective communication and supports the students in their phonological development.

QUESTION 84

Answer: C

Explanation: Providing opportunities for students to listen to and repeat simple words and sentences allows them to practice blending sounds in a meaningful context. This reinforces their phonemic awareness and helps them develop their blending skills, which are essential for accurate pronunciation and reading fluency. It also provides a supportive and engaging environment for young learners to develop their phonological abilities.

QUESTION 85

Answer: C

Explanation: Engaging students in activities that involve analyzing the meanings and functions of prefixes and suffixes in context helps develop their morphological awareness. Understanding the role of prefixes and suffixes in word formation supports vocabulary development and enhances overall language proficiency. By exploring the morphological aspects of words, students can better grasp the meanings of unfamiliar words they encounter.

QUESTION 86

Answer: C

Explanation: Exposing students to irregular plurals in context and providing them with opportunities to practice using these forms is crucial for understanding and internalizing these patterns. Engaging activities, such as reading stories or playing games with irregular plural nouns, make the learning process enjoyable and effective. This approach helps young learners become more confident in their use of irregular plurals.

QUESTION 87

Answer: D

Explanation: Engaging students in activities that involve sentence combining and creating sentence variety can help improve their syntax and sentence construction. By practicing various sentence structures, students develop a better understanding of how to craft clear and well-structured sentences, avoiding run-on sentences and enhancing their writing skills.

QUESTION 88

Answer: C

Explanation: Engaging students in activities that involve using context clues to infer word meanings helps develop their semantic understanding and vocabulary skills. This approach encourages students to become active learners and use their surrounding language context to deduce the meanings of unfamiliar words. By doing so, they build a stronger vocabulary foundation and improve their overall language comprehension.

QUESTION 89

Answer: C

Explanation: Teaching students about effective organizational patterns and transitions for speeches can significantly enhance their oral discourse skills. By understanding how to structure their presentations logically and use smooth transitions between ideas, students can maintain coherence and keep their audience engaged. This approach empowers learners to deliver more effective and impactful public speeches.

QUESTION 90

Answer: C

Explanation: Teaching students about different types of linking devices and how to use them effectively helps improve their written discourse skills. Linking words and phrases, such as "however," "in addition," and "therefore," enhance the coherence of paragraphs and help convey connections between ideas. By mastering these linking devices, students can create more cohesive and well-structured written texts.

QUESTION 91

Answer: C

Explanation: Creating a culturally inclusive learning community involves recognizing and valuing the cultural diversity of students. By celebrating and leveraging their diverse backgrounds, educators can create a positive and engaging environment that enhances language learning and academic achievement.

QUESTION 92

Answer: C

Explanation: Incorporating diverse perspectives and materials in the curriculum helps students develop a broader understanding of the world and encourages critical thinking by exposing them to various viewpoints and cultural experiences.

QUESTION 93

Answer: C

Explanation: Fostering a sense of belonging and inclusivity involves creating a classroom environment where students can share their cultures and learn from one another. This helps build positive relationships and promotes mutual respect among students.

QUESTION 94

Answer: D

Explanation: The transitional bilingual program aims to provide instruction in both the students' native language and English, gradually transitioning them to English-only instruction as their language proficiency improves.

QUESTION 95

Answer: C

Explanation: The dual-language program model aims to develop students' proficiency in two languages, usually their native language and English, while also fostering academic achievement.

QUESTION 96

Answer: D

Explanation: Immersion programs immerse students in an English-speaking environment, which encourages rapid language acquisition by exposing students to the language in authentic contexts.

QUESTION 97

Answer: C

Explanation: The Audio-Lingual Method places a strong emphasis on drilling and repetitive practice of grammatical structures to develop accurate language production.

QUESTION 98

Answer: C

Explanation: TBLT focuses on real-life tasks that require communication, promoting the use of language in meaningful contexts to develop practical language skills.

QUESTION 99

Answer: B

Explanation: The Grammar-Translation Method was criticized for prioritizing translation and rote memorization of vocabulary and rules, often at the expense of effective communication in the target language.

QUESTION 100

Answer: B

Explanation: Formative assessments are used to monitor student progress, provide timely feedback, and make instructional decisions to enhance learning.

QUESTION 101

Answer: C

Explanation: Differentiation involves tailoring instruction to accommodate the varying readiness levels, learning styles, and interests of students.

QUESTION 102

Answer: C

Explanation: Summative assessments are used to evaluate overall student achievement and inform broader decisions about curriculum design and instructional strategies.

QUESTION 103

Answer: C

Explanation: By implementing group discussions that value and accommodate different communication preferences, you create an inclusive environment where students feel comfortable expressing their opinions, regardless of their cultural background.

QUESTION 104

Answer: D

Explanation: Fostering a culturally inclusive environment involves recognizing and respecting different communication and collaboration styles. Developing strategies that accommodate both individualist and collectivist preferences promotes effective collaboration among all students.

QUESTION 105

Answer: B

Explanation: It's important to address students' concerns and modify activities when needed to avoid perpetuating stereotypes or causing discomfort. Modifying the activity to promote genuine cultural awareness and understanding is a respectful and inclusive approach.

QUESTION 106

Answer: C

Explanation: Creating a safe and supportive environment is crucial for language development and well-being. By addressing the emotional impact of discrimination and providing a nurturing classroom, you can help the student develop language skills while fostering a sense of belonging.

QUESTION 107

Answer: C

Explanation: Challenging negative stereotypes and providing positive reinforcement can boost the student's self-confidence and motivation to learn. Encouraging a growth mindset and fostering a supportive environment are key to overcoming language challenges.

QUESTION 108

Answer: C

Explanation: Providing opportunities for the student to share their culture and experiences not only celebrates their uniqueness but also helps them feel valued and confident. This approach fosters a positive environment that encourages participation and language development.

QUESTION 109

Answer: C

Explanation: Raising awareness of different communication styles and equipping students with strategies for effective cross-cultural communication enhances understanding and reduces potential misunderstandings.

QUESTION 110

Answer: C

Explanation: Valuing and accommodating both communication styles promotes an inclusive environment and enhances students' ability to effectively communicate across cultural boundaries.

QUESTION 111

Answer: C

Explanation: Nonverbal cues can vary across cultures, and it's important to avoid making assumptions. By discussing cultural differences and encouraging open communication, you create an environment where all students feel valued and understood.

QUESTION 112

Answer: C

Explanation: By implementing group discussions that value and accommodate different communication preferences, you create an inclusive environment where students feel comfortable expressing their opinions, regardless of their cultural background.

QUESTION 113

Answer: C

Explanation: Addressing conflicts through respectful dialogue allows students to understand and appreciate each other's cultural perspectives, promoting empathy and contributing to a culturally inclusive learning community.

QUESTION 114

Answer: C

Explanation: Providing a range of activity options empowers students to engage in tasks that align with their cultural preferences, fostering inclusivity and enhancing their language learning experience.

QUESTION 115

Answer: C

Explanation: Cross-cultural differences can lead to misinterpretation of nonverbal cues, such as gestures, facial expressions, and body language. Students from different cultural backgrounds may have distinct ways of expressing emotions or attitudes, which can sometimes lead to misunderstandings in the classroom.

QUESTION 116

Answer: B

Explanation: Understanding the values and beliefs of students' cultures allows teachers to create an inclusive and supportive learning environment. By valuing and respecting students' cultural backgrounds, teachers can better cater to their diverse needs and foster a positive classroom atmosphere that promotes learning and growth.

QUESTION 117

Answer: D

Explanation: Incorporating culturally responsive teaching practices is an effective strategy for addressing cross-cultural differences in the classroom. This approach acknowledges and values students' diverse cultural backgrounds, integrating their experiences and perspectives into the curriculum, and promoting a more meaningful and relevant learning experience for all students.

QUESTION 118

Answer: B

Explanation: Cultural identity can positively influence language development in second language learners by creating a sense of belonging and motivation to learn the second language. When students feel connected to their cultural identity, they are more likely to be interested in and engaged with the language learning process, leading to better language acquisition outcomes.

QUESTION 119

Answer: C

Explanation: Racism and discrimination can have a significant impact on language learning and academic achievement for English language learners. Experiencing racism and discrimination can lead to feelings of exclusion and reduce a student's motivation to engage in the learning process, which can hinder their language development and overall academic progress.

QUESTION 120

Answer: C

Explanation: ESL teachers can address the effects of stereotyping in the language learning environment by challenging stereotypes through the use of diverse and inclusive teaching materials. By presenting a wide range of perspectives and experiences, teachers can help students develop a more nuanced understanding of different cultures and combat harmful stereotypes that may hinder language learning and cross-cultural understanding.

QUESTION 121

Answer: A

Explanation: A potential challenge in cross-cultural communication is assuming that all cultures have identical communication styles. Different cultures may have distinct preferences for communication patterns, such as directness, formality, or use of nonverbal cues. Recognizing and adapting to these differences is essential for effective cross-cultural communication.

QUESTION 122

Answer: D

Explanation: Being open-minded and respectful of cultural differences is recommended for effective cross-cultural communication. Showing genuine interest in and respect for different cultural norms and practices can foster a positive and productive communication environment, promoting understanding and cooperation between individuals from diverse backgrounds.

QUESTION 123

Answer: C

Explanation: Misinterpreting nonverbal cues in cross-cultural communication can lead to misunderstandings and conflicts in communication. Different cultures may ascribe different meanings to gestures, facial expressions, and body language, and misinterpretations can result in unintended offenses or breakdowns in communication. Being aware of these differences and practicing cultural sensitivity can help avoid misunderstandings and promote effective cross-cultural communication.

QUESTION 124

Answer: C

Explanation: When recommending an ESOL program model, Maria should consider the language development needs and English proficiency levels of the recently arrived ELLs. Different program models may be more suitable for students at varying levels of English language and literacy development. For students with limited English proficiency, a pull-out model might provide more intensive language support, while those with some language proficiency could benefit from the inclusion model, which allows for language learning in a content-rich environment alongside native English speakers.

QUESTION 125

Answer: C

Explanation: The study's findings might be attributed to the dual-language immersion program's approach, which allows students to use both their native language and English for academic content. In this model, instruction is provided in both languages, promoting bilingualism and biliteracy. This consistent exposure to and use of both languages in meaningful academic contexts likely contributes to students' enhanced academic achievement and bilingual proficiency.

QUESTION 126

Answer: B

Explanation: One of the potential benefits of the newcomer program is that it helps ELLs develop language skills more quickly. The specialized English language instruction provided in the newcomer program targets the specific language needs of recently arrived ELLs, enabling them to acquire English proficiency faster. This intensive language support can accelerate their ability to participate in regular classes with greater confidence and success.

QUESTION 127

Answer: B

Explanation: The CLT approach is more aligned with current language teaching research and best practices. Research indicates that learners benefit from authentic communication and meaningful language use in real-life contexts. The CLT approach fosters communicative competence and encourages students to actively use the language, making it more effective and relevant for language acquisition compared to the Grammar-Translation method, which primarily focuses on grammar rules and translation exercises.

QUESTION 128

Answer: C

Explanation: The key consideration in selecting the appropriate teaching method is the students' specific language learning goals and needs. For students who are preparing for everyday communication in English, the Task-Based Language Teaching (TBLT) approach is likely more suitable. TBLT emphasizes meaningful language use in context, which aligns well with real-life communication needs. The method's focus on completing authentic tasks promotes language fluency and practical language skills, making it beneficial for students aiming to communicate effectively in English.

QUESTION 129

Answer: B

Explanation: The Natural Approach is better supported for developing students' oral language skills. This approach promotes language acquisition through immersion in meaningful and authentic communication situations. Research shows that learners exposed to the target language in relevant contexts have better outcomes in oral language development. The Natural Approach's emphasis on real-life language use and communication allows students to internalize language structures and develop their oral proficiency more effectively than the Direct Method, which primarily focuses on grammar rules and translation.

QUESTION 130

Answer: B

Explanation: When selecting instructional resources for ELLs, it is crucial to choose materials that are culturally relevant and linguistically appropriate for the students. Resources that resonate with the students' cultural backgrounds and language proficiency are more likely to engage learners and facilitate better comprehension.

QUESTION 131

Answer: C

Explanation: Adapting a complex reading passage for beginner ELLs should involve providing support without compromising the core content. Offering a glossary with definitions for key vocabulary words allows students to access the meaning of unfamiliar terms while maintaining the integrity of the original text.

QUESTION 132

Answer: C

Explanation: Designing effective ESOL instructional resources involves tailoring materials to the specific language proficiency levels and learning objectives of the students. This approach ensures that the resources address the needs of the learners and support their language development appropriately.

QUESTION 133

Answer: C

Explanation: Using authentic materials that align with students' interests and experiences can significantly enhance engagement and language acquisition. Relevant materials capture students' attention, making language and content instruction more meaningful and relatable.

QUESTION 134

Answer: C

Explanation: After using multimedia resources, engaging students in discussions and reflections fosters language development. This approach encourages students to express their thoughts, apply new vocabulary, and improve their communication skills.

QUESTION 135

Answer: B

Explanation: Integrating academic vocabulary across different content areas exposes ELLs to specialized language used in various academic disciplines. This strategy enhances their ability to understand and communicate effectively in academic settings, leading to overall language proficiency growth.

QUESTION 136

Answer: C

Explanation: Language learning apps offer personalized learning experiences, allowing students to progress at their own pace. This adaptive approach can cater to individual learning needs and preferences, enhancing student engagement and motivation.

QUESTION 137

Answer: B

Explanation: Video conferencing tools facilitate real-time communication and collaboration, providing ELLs with opportunities to practice language skills in authentic contexts. These interactions mimic real-life language use, improving students' speaking and listening abilities.

QUESTION 138

Answer: A

Explanation: A diverse range of online resources should be used to address different language skills and cater to various learning styles. Relying solely on one type of online resource may not effectively meet the needs of all learners and may limit their language development opportunities.

QUESTION 139

Answer: B

Explanation: Using multimedia resources engages students through visual and auditory input, making the content more accessible to diverse learners. Interactive websites and videos can provide context, promote discussions, and support language development, fostering a deeper understanding of the topic.

QUESTION 140

Answer: C

Explanation: Creating a classroom blog allows students to practice writing skills, share their ideas, and interact with classmates in a digital format. This strategy promotes authentic language use, encourages collaboration, and enhances students' written expression.

QUESTION 141

Answer: B

Explanation: Integrating online language learning platforms with interactive exercises provides students with independent learning opportunities. These platforms often offer engaging activities, immediate feedback, and personalized learning experiences, which can enhance students' language proficiency outside of the classroom.

QUESTION 142

Answer: B

Explanation: Utilizing digital flashcards with audio pronunciations provides a multisensory learning experience. Students can see the words, hear the correct pronunciation, and reinforce their understanding through repeated exposure, promoting effective vocabulary acquisition.

QUESTION 143

Answer: C

Explanation: Using video conferencing tools allows ELLs to engage in authentic conversations with native English speakers, providing real-life listening and speaking practice. This strategy exposes students to different accents, communication styles, and cultural interactions, enhancing their language skills.

QUESTION 144

Answer: B

Explanation: Integrating online collaborative platforms allows ELLs to work together on projects, share ideas, and engage in discussions. This technology-based strategy promotes creativity, critical thinking, and teamwork among students, leading to a richer and more interactive learning experience.

QUESTION 145

Answer: A

Explanation: The approach of giving the same test at the beginning and end of the semester allows Julie to compare students' performance over time. This helps identify growth or changes in language proficiency, indicating the reliability of the assessment in measuring progress.

QUESTION 146

Answer: B

Explanation: Using a mix of assessment types allows Mr. Johnson to measure different language skills and provides a more comprehensive evaluation of students' language proficiency. This approach enhances the validity of the assessments, as it aligns with the diverse language needs of his students.

QUESTION 147

Answer: B

Explanation: The correlation between the test scores and students' classroom performance indicates the reliability of the proficiency test. A high correlation suggests that the test accurately reflects students' language abilities and predicts their performance in real-life language use situations.

QUESTION 148

Answer: B

Explanation: An oral proficiency interview assesses a student's ability to communicate effectively in spoken language, which is a crucial skill for English Language Learners. It provides a more authentic measure of a student's language skills compared to traditional written tests.

QUESTION 149

Answer: B

Explanation: Reliability refers to the consistency of assessment results when the same test is administered to the same group of students on different occasions. It ensures that the instrument provides consistent measurements of students' abilities.

QUESTION 150

Answer: C

Explanation: Performance-based assessments involve tasks that mirror real-life situations, requiring students to use their language skills in context. This type of assessment provides insights into how well students can apply their language knowledge and skills.

QUESTION 151

Answer: C

Explanation: Formative assessment is used to monitor students' progress during instruction, providing feedback that helps teachers adjust their teaching strategies to better meet students' needs.

QUESTION 152

Answer: C

Explanation: Communicating assessment results effectively involves presenting information in a way that is easily understandable for stakeholders, using clear language, visuals, and context to convey the implications of the data.

QUESTION 153

Answer: B

Explanation: Summative assessments are designed to measure students' overall performance and achievement at the end of a specific period, such as a unit or a course. These assessments are often used to make decisions about students' progress and program effectiveness.

QUESTION 154

Answer: C

Explanation: Using multiple measures of assessment, which may include various types of assessments, offers a well-rounded understanding of students' language proficiency and content knowledge, taking into account different aspects of their abilities.

QUESTION 155

Answer: C

Explanation: When aligning assessments with language and content standards, teachers should ensure that assessments reflect the language skills needed to access and demonstrate understanding of the content being taught.

QUESTION 156

Answer: C

Explanation: Ongoing assessment helps teachers monitor students' growth and adapt their teaching strategies to address individual needs. This continuous feedback loop enhances the effectiveness of ESOL instruction.

QUESTION 157

Answer: C

Explanation: Standardized tests may not accurately assess ELL students' content knowledge due to language barriers, focusing primarily on language skills rather than the depth of their understanding of subject matter.

QUESTION 158

Answer: B

Explanation: Language bias in standardized tests can unfairly disadvantage ELLs. When interpreting results, it's crucial to make fair comparisons by considering language proficiency and making necessary adjustments.

QUESTION 159

Answer: C

Explanation: Interpreting assessment results for ELLs requires a holistic approach. By considering a variety of data sources, educators gain a better understanding of students' strengths, needs, and progress in both language and content areas.

QUESTION 160

Answer: C

Explanation: Effective communication of assessment results involves providing parents and students with understandable information about their performance. Clear explanations help stakeholders understand the results and how they relate to students' progress and areas for improvement.

QUESTION 161

Answer: C

Explanation: Carlos should design assessments that reflect both the content standards for science and the language skills necessary to demonstrate understanding. This approach ensures that students' language abilities are integrated into the assessment while still assessing their knowledge of the content.

QUESTION 162

Answer: C

Explanation: When interpreting standardized test scores for ELLs, it's important to consider the influence of language on the results. Language barriers can affect ELLs' performance, and it's crucial to account for their language proficiency when evaluating their scores.

QUESTION 163

Answer: A

Explanation: Brown v. Board of Education was a landmark Supreme Court decision in 1954 that declared racial segregation in public schools unconstitutional. This decision played a crucial role in shaping ESOL programs as it led to increased efforts to provide equitable educational opportunities for ELLs, eliminating segregation and discrimination based on language barriers.

QUESTION 164

Answer: A

Explanation: The No Child Left Behind Act (NCLB), passed in 2001, is a federal law that provides funding and guidelines to support English Language Learners' education. It requires schools to assess ELLs' language proficiency and academic progress and holds them accountable for the academic achievement of these students.

QUESTION 165

Answer: A

Explanation: The Supreme Court decision in Lau v. Nichols ruled that schools must provide English Language Learners with appropriate language assistance to ensure they have equal access to education. As a result, this decision led to the establishment of bilingual education programs, where instruction is provided in both the students' native language and English, facilitating their academic development.

QUESTION 166

Answer: C

Explanation: The SMART goal-setting framework (Specific, Measurable, Achievable, Relevant, Time-bound) is an effective strategy for ESL teachers to set achievable and focused professional goals. This approach helps teachers define clear objectives, identify measurable outcomes, and establish a realistic timeline for accomplishing their goals.

QUESTION 167

Answer: C

Explanation: Engaging in cross-disciplinary workshops and collaborating with teachers from various subject areas can provide valuable insights and diverse perspectives. This exposure allows ESL teachers to learn new teaching strategies and adapt them to their ESOL classrooms, fostering their professional growth.

QUESTION 168

Answer: D

Explanation: Enrolling in a TESOL certification program would be the most relevant and beneficial professional development activity for an ESL teacher aiming to improve classroom language instruction. Such a program focuses specifically on enhancing language teaching skills and strategies, providing valuable insights and knowledge for teaching English to non-native speakers.

QUESTION 169

Answer: C

Explanation: Effective collaboration between ESL teachers and content-area teachers involves providing the latter with language support strategies. By sharing techniques for modifying instruction and scaffolding content to make it accessible to ELLs, content-area teachers can better meet the needs of their diverse students, ensuring comprehensive and challenging educational opportunities.

QUESTION 170

Answer: B

Explanation: Technology can be a valuable tool for enhancing collaboration between ESL teachers and content-area teachers. Video conferencing platforms allow for real-time communication, making it easier for educators to discuss lesson planning, student progress, and strategies for supporting ELLs, even when they are physically distant.

QUESTION 171

Answer: C

Explanation: Creating interdisciplinary teams that consist of both ESL and content-area teachers fosters collaboration and a comprehensive approach to supporting ELLs. Through these teams, educators can work together, share expertise, and develop strategies that align with the needs of English Language Learners, leading to more effective and holistic educational opportunities.

QUESTION 172

Answer: B

Explanation: As an ESOL resource, offering workshops on content-specific topics to classroom teachers can be highly beneficial. By providing strategies for modifying instruction and supporting ELLs in their classrooms, the ESOL resource teacher can empower classroom teachers to create inclusive learning environments for English Language Learners.

QUESTION 173

Answer: B

Explanation: An ESOL resource teacher can make a significant impact on the school community by actively participating in school-wide committees and professional development activities. This involvement allows them to share their expertise, advocate for the needs of English Language Learners, and collaborate with colleagues to improve educational opportunities for all students.

QUESTION 174

Answer: C

Explanation: Effective communication with parents of English Language Learners involves organizing parent-teacher conferences and providing translation services when necessary. This approach demonstrates respect for the parents' language and cultural background, fostering a positive and inclusive partnership between the school and the families of ELLs.

QUESTION 175

Answer: B

Explanation: Brown v. Board of Education was a landmark Supreme Court decision that ruled racial segregation in public schools unconstitutional. This decision paved the way for educational reforms and impacted ESOL programs by promoting the integration of English Language Learners into regular classrooms, ensuring equal access to quality education for all students, regardless of their language background.

QUESTION 176

Answer: A

Explanation: The No Child Left Behind Act (NCLB) is a federal legislation that aims to improve the educational achievement of all students, including English Language Learners. NCLB provides funding for ESOL programs and requires schools to assess and report the progress of ELLs. It holds schools accountable for the academic performance of these students and encourages the use of research-based strategies to support their language development and academic success.

QUESTION 177

Answer: C

Explanation: The Supreme Court decision in Lau v. Nichols ruled that schools must provide English Language Learners with appropriate language assistance to ensure equal access to education. As a result, this decision led to the establishment of bilingual education programs, where instruction is provided in both the students' native language and English, to facilitate their academic development.

QUESTION 178

Answer: C

Explanation: The SMART goal-setting framework (Specific, Measurable, Achievable, Relevant, Time-bound) is an effective approach for setting professional goals. By applying this strategy, Ms. Jackson can define clear and specific objectives, identify measurable outcomes, ensure goals are achievable, align them with her teaching context, and set a realistic timeline for accomplishing them.

QUESTION 179

Answer: C

Explanation: Engaging in cross-disciplinary workshops and collaborating with teachers from various subject areas can be highly beneficial for Ms. Jackson's professional growth. These experiences expose her to diverse perspectives and teaching strategies, enabling her to adapt and incorporate effective approaches into her ESL classroom.

QUESTION 180

Answer: D

Explanation: Pursuing a TESOL certification program aligns best with Ms. Jackson's goal of improving classroom language instruction. This program provides her with specialized training and strategies to effectively teach English to non-native speakers, helping her enhance her language instruction skills and support her English Language Learners more effectively.

QUESTION 181

Answer: B

Explanation: Effective collaboration between Mr. Lee and content-area teachers involves providing the latter with language support strategies. By sharing techniques for modifying instruction and scaffolding content to make it accessible to ELLs, content-area teachers can better meet the needs of their diverse students, ensuring comprehensive and challenging educational opportunities.

QUESTION 182

Answer: C

Explanation: Offering professional development workshops on ELL instructional strategies can help address the challenge of content-area teachers being hesitant to modify their lessons. By providing targeted training and support, Mr. Lee can empower his colleagues with practical tools and techniques for effectively instructing English Language Learners in their classrooms.

QUESTION 183

Answer: B

Explanation: Technology can be a valuable tool for enhancing collaboration between Mr. Lee and content-area teachers. Video conferencing platforms allow for real-time communication, making it easier for educators to discuss lesson planning, student progress, and strategies for supporting ELLs, even when they are physically distant.

QUESTION 184

Answer: B

Explanation: As an ESOL resource, offering workshops on content-specific topics to classroom teachers can be highly beneficial. By providing strategies for modifying instruction and supporting ELLs in their classrooms, Mrs. Smith can empower classroom teachers to create inclusive learning environments for English Language Learners.

QUESTION 185

Answer: B

Explanation: As the ESOL resource teacher, Mrs. Smith can make a significant impact on the school community by actively participating in school-wide committees and professional development activities. This involvement allows her to share her expertise, advocate for the needs of English Language Learners, and collaborate with colleagues to improve educational opportunities for all students.

QUESTION 186

Answer: C

Explanation: Effective communication with parents of English Language Learners involves organizing parent-teacher conferences and providing translation services when necessary. This approach demonstrates respect for the parents' language and cultural background, fostering a positive and inclusive partnership between the school and the families of ELLs.

QUESTION 187

Answer: C

Explanation: Performance-based tasks, such as projects, presentations, and demonstrations, allow English Language Learners to showcase their understanding of content-area concepts actively. These tasks require them to apply their knowledge, which can provide more meaningful insights into their comprehension compared to simple recall-based tests like true/false or fill-in-the-blank.

QUESTION 188

Answer: B

Explanation: When an English Language Learner performs well in oral discussions but struggles with written assessments, it may indicate a language barrier affecting their writing abilities. The teacher should consider providing additional support and scaffolding to help the student improve their written language skills.

QUESTION 189

Answer: A

Explanation: Formative assessment is designed to monitor students' progress and understanding throughout the learning process. It helps teachers identify areas of improvement and adjust instruction accordingly. For English Language Learners, formative assessments are particularly useful as they allow ongoing feedback and support to ensure continuous development in content-area learning.

QUESTION 190

Answer: B

Explanation: Content-based instruction focuses on teaching language skills while simultaneously addressing content-area knowledge. A key feature is the use of authentic materials relevant to the subject being taught. This approach helps English Language Learners engage with real-world content, which enhances their language learning experience.

QUESTION 191

Answer: D

Explanation: The primary goal of sheltered instruction is to make content-area instruction comprehensible for English Language Learners while simultaneously developing their language skills. Teachers use various instructional strategies and scaffolding techniques to help ELLs understand academic content and participate actively in the learning process.

QUESTION 192

Answer: D

Explanation: In content-based language instruction, language objectives are integrated with content objectives. They are designed to support ELLs' language development by emphasizing the language skills necessary for understanding and expressing knowledge related to the content being taught. These objectives ensure that language learning is meaningful and relevant to the subject matter.

QUESTION 193

Answer: C

Explanation: Providing English Language Learners with opportunities for authentic language use in meaningful contexts enhances their academic language proficiency. Engaging students in discussions, debates, presentations, and real-world tasks allows them to practice using academic language naturally and effectively.

QUESTION 194

Answer: C

Explanation: Visual aids and graphic organizers serve as powerful tools to support English Language Learners' comprehension and organization of information in content-area instruction. They provide a visual representation of concepts, making complex information more accessible and facilitating understanding for ELLs.

QUESTION 195

Answer: C

Explanation: Breaking complex content-area tasks into smaller, manageable steps is an effective scaffolding strategy for English Language Learners. This approach allows ELLs to focus on one aspect of the task at a time, reducing feelings of overwhelm and facilitating successful completion of the assignment.

QUESTION 196

Answer: D

Explanation: Phonics-based activities help ELLs decode and recognize written words by teaching them the relationship between letters and their sounds. This strategy aids in building their reading skills and increasing their word recognition abilities.

QUESTION 197

Answer: C

Explanation: Providing model texts and examples exposes ELLs to various writing styles, structures, and language patterns, which can broaden their understanding of effective writing and aid in their own writing development.

QUESTION 198

Answer: D

Explanation: Graphic organizers visually represent ideas and concepts, helping ELLs to plan and organize their thoughts before writing. This process supports their writing development by providing structure and clarity.

QUESTION 199

Answer: C

Explanation: Annotating and highlighting key points while reading encourages active engagement with the content, helps ELLs identify important information, and improves comprehension.

QUESTION 200

Answer: C

Explanation: Pre-teaching vocabulary helps ELLs understand and engage with the academic text, enabling them to grasp the content more effectively and engage in deeper comprehension.

QUESTION 201

Answer: D

Explanation: Identifying emotional cues and context clues allows ELLs to infer emotions and intentions in written texts, contributing to their ability to comprehend social nuances and deeper meanings.

QUESTION 202

Answer: C

Explanation: Modeling the process of constructing an essay provides ELLs with a clear framework for organizing their ideas, supporting them in developing effective writing skills for academic purposes.

QUESTION 203

Answer: C

Explanation: Peer feedback offers ELLs diverse perspectives and constructive criticism, helping them refine their writing skills and promoting a collaborative approach to improvement.

QUESTION 204

Answer: C

Explanation: Integrating real-world writing tasks helps ELLs see the practical relevance of writing skills in their daily lives, enhancing their motivation and engagement in the writing process.

QUESTION 205

Answer: C

Explanation: Engaging English Language Learners in interactive listening activities with visual aids helps scaffold their understanding and provides contextual support. Visual aids can include images, diagrams, or video clips that enhance comprehension and make the listening experience more meaningful.

QUESTION 206

Answer: A

Explanation: English Language Learners may face challenges when exposed to diverse accents and speech rates in authentic communication situations. This can affect their ability to comprehend and follow spoken language, as they may not be accustomed to variations in pronunciation and pacing.

QUESTION 207

Answer: A

Explanation: Encouraging note-taking while listening to lectures or audio materials encourages active engagement and helps English Language Learners process and retain information. Note-taking also reinforces their listening skills and aids in better understanding the content being presented.

QUESTION 208

Answer: C

Explanation: Engaging English Language Learners in authentic and meaningful conversations provides them with real-world language practice. This approach helps develop their speaking skills in natural contexts and enhances their ability to communicate effectively in various academic situations.

QUESTION 209

Answer: C

Explanation: Providing opportunities for small group discussions allows English Language Learners to practice speaking in a supportive and non-threatening environment. This encourages them to engage actively, gain confidence, and receive constructive feedback from peers, leading to improved speaking skills.

QUESTION 210

Answer: D

Explanation: Recording and evaluating oral presentations allows ESL teachers to assess English Language Learners' speaking proficiency more accurately. By listening to recorded speeches, teachers can focus on various aspects of spoken language, such as pronunciation, fluency, and vocabulary usage.

QUESTION 211

Answer: C

Explanation: Assessing English Language Learners' reading comprehension using authentic texts relevant to their interests provides a meaningful context for evaluation. It helps engage students and encourages them to apply reading strategies to texts that resonate with their experiences and preferences.

QUESTION 212

Answer: D

Explanation: Providing opportunities for rereading and reflection during reading assessments allows English Language Learners to improve their comprehension. It helps them revisit challenging sections, clarify doubts, and deepen their understanding of the text.

QUESTION 213

Answer: C

Explanation: Allowing English Language Learners to choose their reading materials based on their interests enhances intrinsic motivation for reading. When students are engaged with topics that personally appeal to them, they are more likely to be invested in the reading process and experience a greater sense of enjoyment and achievement.

QUESTION 214

Answer: C

Explanation: Assessing both content and language proficiency in English Language Learners' writing allows teachers to provide comprehensive feedback. By evaluating the ideas and organization alongside language usage, teachers can identify areas for improvement and support students' overall writing development.

QUESTION 215

Answer: C

Explanation: Using rubrics with clear criteria and expectations helps English Language Learners understand what is expected in their writing and allows for consistent and fair evaluation. This approach highlights their strengths and areas for improvement, fostering a more productive writing learning process.

QUESTION 216

Answer: D

Explanation: Encouraging self-expression and creativity in English Language Learners' writing helps them develop their unique voice and style in English. This approach fosters confidence, motivation, and a sense of ownership over their writing, leading to more engaged and skilled writers.

QUESTION 217

Answer: C

Explanation: Research shows that providing ELLs with exposure to authentic and context-rich materials, such as texts, videos, and real-life conversations, is an effective vocabulary instruction strategy. This approach allows ELLs to learn vocabulary in meaningful contexts, making it easier for them to understand and use the words in their speaking, listening, reading, and writing activities.

QUESTION 218

Answer: B

Explanation: Engaging ELLs in peer discussions to explain new vocabulary words promotes active learning and deeper understanding. When ELLs have to explain the meaning of a word to their peers, they develop a deeper grasp of the word's usage and context, which can positively impact their reading and writing skills.

QUESTION 219

Answer: B

Explanation: Research indicates that using visual aids, such as pictures and real-life objects, helps ELLs comprehend and remember new words more effectively. Visual support enhances the learners' understanding and retention of vocabulary, which can improve their listening skills as they encounter these words in different contexts.

QUESTION 220

Answer: C

Explanation: One-on-one interviews provide an opportunity to directly assess students' oral language development in a more authentic setting. Through conversations, the teacher can gauge the students' speaking fluency, pronunciation, vocabulary usage, and ability to engage in meaningful communication.

QUESTION 221

Answer: B

Explanation: A listening comprehension exercise with multiple-choice questions allows the teacher to assess ELLs' ability to comprehend spoken English and their understanding of key information. This type of assessment directly targets aural language development and helps identify any areas where students may need additional support.

QUESTION 222

Answer: B

Explanation: Observing and recording ELLs' participation in class discussions over time provides a more comprehensive and continuous assessment of their oral language development. This method allows the teacher to track progress, identify areas for improvement, and make informed instructional decisions to support the students' language development.

QUESTION 223

Answer: D

Explanation: Playing audio recordings of authentic social interactions, such as conversations, interviews, or dialogues, along with accompanying transcripts, helps ELLs develop their listening skills for real-life social purposes. The transcripts provide valuable support for comprehension, allowing students to follow along, identify new vocabulary, and understand the context of the interactions.

QUESTION 224

Answer: C

Explanation: Role-playing activities that simulate everyday social interactions allow ELLs to practice and improve their listening skills in a meaningful and context-rich setting. Through these activities, students can engage in realistic conversations, pay attention to social cues, and develop their ability to comprehend spoken language in social contexts.

QUESTION 225

Answer: C

Explanation: Interactive listening tasks, where ELLs actively engage with the listening material through discussions, role-plays, and follow-up activities, promote active listening skills. Passive listening, like listening to radio programs without interaction, does not provide the same level of engagement and practice in understanding and responding to spoken English in social settings.

QUESTION 226

Answer: C

Explanation: Engaging ELLs in group discussions on topics that are relevant and meaningful to them allows for authentic and interactive communication. This instructional practice provides opportunities for ELLs to practice their speaking skills, exchange ideas, and learn from their peers, which enhances their ability to communicate effectively for various social purposes.

QUESTION 227

Answer: B

Explanation: Creating a supportive and safe environment is essential for helping ELLs feel comfortable and confident when speaking in English. Fear of making mistakes or being judged can hinder language development, so providing a positive and non-threatening atmosphere encourages ELLs to take risks and improve their speaking skills without anxiety.

QUESTION 228

Answer: C

Explanation: Meaningful and interactive pair or group discussions promote authentic communication among ELLs. Engaging in dialogues with peers allows them to practice speaking in real-life situations and collaborate in English conversations, fostering their speaking skills and strategies for various social purposes.

QUESTION 229

Answer: C

Explanation: Encouraging collaborative activities and group projects allows ELLs to engage with their peers, practice language skills, and build a sense of community, fostering a student-centered learning environment.

QUESTION 230

Answer: C

Explanation: Incorporating culturally diverse materials and experiences helps ELLs feel valued and respected, and it creates a more inclusive and supportive learning community.

QUESTION 231

Answer: C

Explanation: Adapting instruction to meet diverse learning needs ensures that ELLs receive the support and resources they need to succeed, promoting a student-centered approach.

QUESTION 232

Answer: C

Explanation: Incorporating visuals and gestures helps make language input more understandable and accessible to ELLs, enhancing their language development.

QUESTION 233

Answer: C

Explanation: Encouraging peer discussions and partner activities provides ELLs with opportunities to practice speaking and listening skills, contributing to their language development.

QUESTION 234

Answer: C

Explanation: Providing specific praise and constructive suggestions helps ELLs understand their strengths and areas for improvement, supporting their language development.

QUESTION 235

Answer: B

Explanation: Tailoring instruction to the individual needs and backgrounds of SIFE students acknowledges their unique challenges and helps bridge educational gaps.

QUESTION 236

Answer: C

Explanation: Implementing differentiated instruction and accommodations ensures that ELLs with special needs receive appropriate support, fostering their language development.

QUESTION 237

Answer: B

Explanation: Offering enrichment opportunities and challenging activities supports gifted and talented ELLs in further developing their language skills while nurturing their advanced abilities.

QUESTION 238

Answer: C

Explanation: Fostering open communication and valuing diverse perspectives help ELLs feel a sense of belonging and create a supportive learning community.

QUESTION 239

Answer: C

Explanation: Acknowledging and respecting diverse cultural backgrounds fosters inclusivity and helps create a student-centered learning environment for ELLs.

QUESTION 240

Answer: C

Explanation: Integrating technology tools that support language acquisition and collaboration enhances the student-centered learning experience for ELLs.

QUESTION 241

Answer: C

Explanation: Incorporating authentic materials provides ELLs with exposure to real-world language usage and meaningful context, enhancing language development.

QUESTION 242

Answer: C

Explanation: Integrating authentic tasks like role-plays and simulations allows ELLs to use language in real-life scenarios, promoting practical language skills.

QUESTION 243

Answer: C

Explanation: Scaffolding involves providing temporary support and guidance to ELLs, helping them build language skills and achieve success.

QUESTION 244

Answer: B

Explanation: Offering varied tasks and materials based on individual proficiency levels allows ELLs to receive appropriate support and challenge.

QUESTION 245

Answer: C

Explanation: Implementing targeted interventions and building foundational skills helps ELLs with limited prior formal education develop necessary language and academic abilities.

QUESTION 246

Answer: B

Explanation: Providing opportunities for enrichment and challenging activities supports the language development of gifted and talented ELLs while nurturing their exceptional abilities.

QUESTION 247

Answer: C

Explanation: Icebreaker activities are designed to help students get to know each other and the teacher, creating a positive and inclusive classroom environment. This supports the development of a supportive learning community.

QUESTION 248

Answer: C

Explanation: Incorporating culturally relevant materials and topics helps engage students and allows them to connect their own experiences and backgrounds to the content. It promotes cultural awareness and inclusivity.

QUESTION 249

Answer: C

Explanation: Providing clear guidelines for using English during group activities helps create an environment where ELLs are encouraged to communicate in English, supporting language development and interaction.

QUESTION 250

Answer: D

Explanation: Summarizing a passage in their own words requires students to use writing skills to process and express the main ideas, demonstrating comprehension of the reading material.

QUESTION 251

Answer: C

Explanation: Comprehensible input is language that is understandable to learners, allowing them to grasp new concepts and language structures while engaging in meaningful communication.

QUESTION 252

Answer: C

Explanation: Engaging students in a role-playing conversation provides an opportunity for authentic spoken interaction, allowing the teacher to assess their speaking skills and language use in context.

QUESTION 253

Answer: C

Explanation: Conducting a language assessment helps determine the student's language proficiency and academic needs, allowing you to provide targeted support and appropriate instructional strategies.

QUESTION 254

Answer: C

Explanation: Differentiating instruction for a gifted and talented ELL involves providing more challenging and enriching activities that cater to the student's advanced skills and abilities.

QUESTION 255

Answer: C

Explanation: Providing simplified texts, visual aids, and targeted reading strategies helps scaffold the student's comprehension and create a more accessible learning experience, addressing their special needs.

QUESTION 256

Answer: B

Explanation: By actively using the new vocabulary words in sentences during class discussions, ELLs have the opportunity to contextualize and apply the words in meaningful ways. This process reinforces their understanding and retention of the words, making it an effective vocabulary instruction strategy.

QUESTION 257

Answer: A

Explanation: It is essential to prioritize complex academic vocabulary that ELLs are likely to encounter in different subjects and academic contexts. By introducing them to these terms, ELLs can better understand and participate in classroom discussions and assignments, ultimately supporting their overall language development.

QUESTION 258

Answer: C

Explanation: Interactive and hands-on activities provide meaningful and engaging opportunities for ELLs to use the new vocabulary in various contexts. By using the words actively, ELLs are more likely to retain and internalize the vocabulary, leading to better listening, speaking, reading, and writing development.

QUESTION 259

Answer: B

Explanation: Individual speaking interviews provide direct and personalized insights into each ELL's oral language development. It allows the teacher to assess their fluency, pronunciation, vocabulary usage, and overall communication skills, giving a comprehensive understanding of their progress in English.

QUESTION 260

Answer: D

Explanation: Listening comprehension activities with questions assess the ELLs' ability to understand spoken English and their comprehension skills. This type of assessment directly targets their aural language development and helps identify areas for improvement.

QUESTION 261

Answer: B

Explanation: Playing an audio recording and then asking comprehension questions afterward directly assesses the students' listening skills. It helps the teacher understand their ability to comprehend spoken English, making it an appropriate assessment strategy for evaluating their listening development.

QUESTION262

Answer: C

Explanation: Using authentic audio materials that reflect real-life conversations and natural language helps ELLs develop listening skills for informal social purposes. This approach exposes them to various accents, colloquialisms, and language variations used in everyday interactions, supporting their comprehension and communication abilities.

QUESTION 263

Answer: C

Explanation: Encouraging students to ask questions during lectures promotes active listening. It shows that the teacher values their engagement and encourages them to seek clarification or express their thoughts. Active listening involves interactive communication and deeper engagement with the content being presented.

QUESTION 264

Answer: C

Explanation: Listening to academic lectures and taking notes is an effective activity to develop listening skills for academic purposes. This activity requires students to focus, extract important information, and organize it coherently in their notes, which mirrors the skills needed to comprehend complex academic content.

QUESTION 265

Answer: C

Explanation: In this situation, it's essential to foster an inclusive and supportive learning environment. Option C is the correct answer because encouraging the confident student to involve the hesitant student by asking open-ended questions helps create a positive social interaction. This approach can empower the hesitant student, boost their confidence, and promote their speaking skills by gradually engaging them in the conversation.

QUESTION 266

Answer: A

Explanation: Option A is the correct answer because role-play activities based on real-life academic scenarios can help ESL students practice and develop their speaking skills for academic purposes. Role-plays provide a supportive environment for students to apply academic language in context, build vocabulary, and develop critical thinking skills while discussing various academic topics.

QUESTION 267

Answer: C

Explanation: Option C is the correct answer because encouraging all students to research and prepare arguments with supporting evidence ensures that each student actively contributes to the debate. This approach fosters critical thinking and speaking skills development for all students, regardless of their initial proficiency level. It also allows reserved students to gain confidence and participate more actively in the debate by relying on their prepared arguments.

QUESTION 268

Answer: D

Explanation: Option D is the correct answer because using authentic academic materials, such as lectures or presentations, exposes students to real-world language use and challenges them to develop their listening skills. Gradually scaffolding the listening tasks allows students to build their comprehension abilities step by step, ensuring they can grasp the content effectively without feeling overwhelmed.

QUESTION 269

Answer: C

Explanation: Option C is the correct answer because providing practice listening tests that replicate the format and structure of the standardized test helps familiarize students with the test's expectations and builds their confidence. Regular practice also allows students to develop effective listening strategies, such as note-taking and identifying key information, which can significantly improve their performance on the actual test.

QUESTION 270

Answer: C

Explanation: Option C is the correct answer because differentiating listening tasks based on students' proficiency levels ensures that each student is challenged at an appropriate level. Tailoring the difficulty allows struggling students to gain confidence and progress while keeping advanced learners engaged and challenged. This approach promotes active learning and helps all students improve their listening skills effectively.

QUESTION 271

Answer: C

Explanation: Option C is the correct answer because providing clear guidelines and criteria for presentations sets expectations and helps students structure their content effectively. Encouraging peer feedback fosters a supportive environment where students can learn from each other and grow their speaking skills constructively. This approach ensures that both confident and shy students have an opportunity to improve their speaking abilities through presentations.

QUESTION 272

Answer: C

Explanation: Option C is the correct answer because providing guidance on organizing arguments, using evidence, and engaging with opposing viewpoints helps students develop critical thinking skills and effective speaking strategies during debates. This approach ensures that students learn to present well-structured and supported arguments, leading to a more meaningful academic discourse in the class.

QUESTION 273

Answer: B

Explanation: Option B is the correct answer because encouraging students to use multimedia elements and interactive activities enhances the effectiveness of their presentations. This approach makes the presentations more engaging, allowing students to practice their speaking skills while using various visual aids and involving the audience interactively. It also helps students effectively convey cultural traditions and customs to their peers, fostering cross-cultural understanding in the class.

QUESTION 274

Answer: C

Explanation: Option C is the correct answer because providing opportunities for students to discuss their reading responses orally or through group discussions allows them to demonstrate their understanding in different ways. Some students may have better speaking skills than writing skills, and this approach enables them to showcase their comprehension effectively. It also provides valuable insights into their reading development beyond written assessments.

QUESTION 275

Answer: D

Explanation: Option D is the correct answer because offering a variety of reading materials that reflect different cultural backgrounds and linguistic levels ensures that students are exposed to diverse vocabulary and language expressions. It helps identify areas of improvement in their reading development and provides a more comprehensive assessment of their overall language proficiency. This approach also promotes cultural inclusivity in the classroom.

QUESTION 276

Answer: C

Explanation: Option C is the correct answer because providing additional support and practice with sample questions similar to the ones on the standardized test can help bridge the gap between in-class activities and test performance. This approach familiarizes students with the test format and expectations, allowing them to apply their improved reading comprehension skills effectively during standardized assessments. It also helps students gain confidence in their abilities and reduces anxiety associated with the test-taking process.

QUESTION 277

Answer: C

Explanation: Holistic scoring rubrics are used to assess writing by considering the overall quality and impression of the piece, rather than evaluating specific elements individually. This approach helps teachers get a sense of the overall effectiveness of the writing.

QUESTION 278

Answer: C

Explanation: Playing rhyming games and identifying initial sounds in words are effective activities for developing phonemic awareness, which is an essential skill for early reading and writing development. These activities help children distinguish and manipulate individual sounds in words.

QUESTION 279

Answer: B

Explanation: Collaborative group reading and discussions encourage English Language Learners to engage with texts both socially and academically. This approach promotes comprehension, vocabulary development, and critical thinking, while also allowing students to interact and share their perspectives.

QUESTION 280

Answer: B

Explanation: Prompts for creative writing encourage English Language Learners to express themselves in various contexts and for different purposes. This activity helps them develop their writing skills, creativity, and ability to adapt their writing style to different social and academic contexts.

QUESTION 281

Answer: C

Explanation: Formative assessment is used to continuously monitor students' learning progress and provide feedback to guide instructional decisions. It helps teachers make adjustments to their teaching methods based on students' needs.

QUESTION282

Answer: B

Explanation: For beginning English Language Learners, using picture books and labeling classroom objects helps to build vocabulary through visual associations. It provides a tangible connection between words and objects, aiding in both vocabulary development and early reading comprehension.

QUESTION 283

Answer: B

Explanation: Offering a diverse range of reading materials that reflect different cultures and perspectives helps English Language Learners connect with the content and develop a broader understanding of various social and academic contexts. This approach also supports cultural sensitivity and inclusivity.

QUESTION 284

Answer: D

Explanation: Using multiple assessment methods allows the teacher to gain a comprehensive understanding of the student's abilities. Relying on a single mode of assessment might not accurately reflect the student's overall proficiency in the content area. By combining written tasks and oral discussions, the teacher can better assess the student's language and concept development.

QUESTION285

Answer: C

Explanation: The sheltered instruction approach involves making academic content comprehensible for ELLs while also providing opportunities for language development. Using visual aids, hands-on activities, and clear explanations helps to scaffold the content and make it more accessible to students with diverse language backgrounds. This approach promotes active engagement and understanding of the subject matter.

QUESTION 286

Answer: C

Explanation: Providing real-world examples and relevant materials helps to make abstract concepts more concrete and understandable for English Language Learners. It creates meaningful connections and context for the content-area concepts, enhancing their comprehension. Simplifying the content too much (option B) may result in a lack of academic rigor, while advanced research projects (option D) might overwhelm the students and hinder their understanding.

QUESTION 287

Answer: C

Explanation: Formative assessment provides ongoing feedback and helps the teacher identify students' strengths and weaknesses in real-time. Classroom discussions and quizzes allow the teacher to gauge the students' understanding of the content and identify specific areas of difficulty. Multiple-choice tests (option A) might not provide detailed insights into their learning needs. Group projects (option B) assess collaboration skills, but they might not directly reveal individual content comprehension. One-on-one tutoring (option D) might be helpful later for targeted support, but formative assessment is crucial for immediate feedback.

QUESTION 288

Answer: C

Explanation: Integrating language and content instruction is a key principle of content-based ESOL lessons. By incorporating vocabulary and language exercises related to the literature content, the students not only improve their language skills but also deepen their understanding of the subject matter. Options A, B, and D do not necessarily focus on integrating language and content, which is essential in a content-based ESOL lesson.

QUESTION 289

Answer: B

Explanation: Using visuals, realia (real-life objects), and hands-on activities provides concrete experiences and context for English Language Learners, making the abstract science concepts more accessible. These strategies support comprehension and language development simultaneously. Option A might be overwhelming for newcomers with limited English proficiency. Option C emphasizes writing skills, which might not be appropriate at this stage. Option D promotes critical thinking, but without sufficient language support, the students may struggle to actively participate in a debate.

QUESTION 290

Answer: C

Explanation: Engaging ELLs in thought-provoking discussions and debates stimulates their critical-thinking abilities by encouraging them to analyze, evaluate, and synthesize information. It fosters higher-order thinking skills and enhances their content-area learning. Option A focuses on lower-level cognitive skills and might not challenge critical thinking. Option B emphasizes memorization rather than analytical thinking. Option D can be helpful, but it might not specifically target critical thinking as effectively as thought-provoking discussions and debates.

QUESTION 291

Answer: C

Explanation: Differentiated instruction involves customizing teaching methods and content to meet the diverse needs of students. By implementing differentiated instruction, the teacher can cater to the unique language proficiency levels and learning styles of each student, thereby promoting their development of important learning skills and strategies. Grouping students solely based on language proficiency (option A) might not consider other factors affecting their learning. Option B can lead to a lack of challenge for some students and stigmatize others. Option D focuses on independent learning, which is valuable, but it doesn't address the varying needs of the diverse group effectively.